CLAIMING YOUR INHERITANCE

A GATEWAY TO A RICH AND FULFILLING LIFE

E. J. Garrison

For workshops, retreats, training sessions, and other appearances, please contact us at

garrisonministry@aol.com.
or mail us at
P.O. Box 081485
Racine, WI 53408
ISBN: 147934382X
EAN: 9781479343829

Manufactured in the United States of America
First Edition

TABLE OF CONTENTS

Chapter 1 **INSPIRATION**
Be Inspired by Your Love for Life 1

Chapter 2 **NIA**
You Are Here for a Purpose 11

Chapter 3 **HEALTH**
Being an Able Vessel... 33

Chapter 4 **ECONOMICS**
Christian Economics in a Capitalistic Society 53

Chapter 5 **RESILIENCE**
Don't Quit... 91

Chapter 6 **INTEGRITY**
Doing the Right Thing.. 103

Chapter 7 **TALENT**
A Gift or a Curse 113

Chapter 8 **ATTITUDE**
Your Attitude Determines Your Altitude............................ 131

Chapter 9 **NURTURE**
Continue to Grow and Glow in Christ................................ 143

Chapter 10 **CHURCH MEMBERSHIP**
God's Filling Station 159

Chapter 11 **ESTEEM**
Developing Your Self-Esteem.. 171

Acknowledgements

Beloved, I am a blessed man. It will take each and every page of this book to acknowledge the many people who have had input in this publication. Why, because this publication is a collection of my life journey, as well as accomplishments, achievements, and knowledge. So, I need to start with God. Although that should be a given, I don't want anyone to doubt where I believe my knowledge, ability, and achievement came from. As you read this book, you will understand.

My entire life is a testimony to a woman of faith (my mom), trusting in God to take over and protect and keep her children. So, thank you Mother, Emily Garrison Mitchell, my double mother who not only gave me my biological birth but also led me to Christ, which resulted in my spiritual birth. She did not stop there but became my drill sergeant (you will understand it later in the book), and was determined to make something of my being, what some labeled, academically challenged.

To all of my siblings, you each have played a major role in my growth and development. To my dad, posthumously, you placed in me what I needed to survive.

Now, what can I say about the village, or all the people that God has placed in my life? If I start naming them, I am sure I will miss many, for I had a legion of angels surrounding me all the days of my life…

Clarence Jones, posthumously, who had me
read the mission of the church;

Dr. Dedria Well Smith, Mildred Goodloe, who
supported me wherever I was in life

Lidia Hibbert, who saw something in me
that I did not see in myself;

Nettie Hanson, Roberta Cadwell and so many other
sisters, who always prayed for me

Carolyn Butts Garrison, posthumously,
the mother of my two beautiful sons;

Emma Jones, who also had that gentle touch

The Reverend Amos Chester, a mentor in ministry;

The Rev. Dr. Joe M. Funchess, a confidante and friend

The Reverend Norman Victor Osborne, a model pastor;

The Reverend Alfred Johnson, who supported me
in my first pastorate

Paul Billingslea, posthumously, who gave me a chance to
enter the Christian Education Ministry;

Marshall who believed in me, before I believe in myself

The Reverend Maurice J. Higginbothan, posthumously,
my pastor who pushed me into the ministry;

Joyce Marie, who suggested that I write;

The Right Reverend John Richard Bryant,
who suggested that I publish what I wrote;

And my sister, Carrie L. Hendricks, who told me that if I did
not write and publish, my children and grandchildren may never
know what I was thinking, and nobody else would benefit;

And oh so many others, please forgive me for not mentioning your
name, but I need to be mindful of the trees that have also
contributed to this publication;

You may ask, why did I mention those who have passed away? Well,
they are still alive and well in my heart and in everything that I do.

Additional Acknowledgements

Advisers

Kenya Carlton
Linda Garrison Carlton, CPA
Ladonna Hendricks Johnson, MD
Regina Smith, PhD

Proofreaders/Editors

Shonell Bacon, MFA
Elizabeth Markham, PhD
Kenneth Yorgan, DC
Lisa Parham

To My Sons

Ernest II and Thomas and grandson Theodore

The sky is your limit
The clouds are ladders for you to climb
The stars are light so that you can find your way
So what are you waiting for
Start climbing

There are storms, there will be many storms
While you are climbing
But you must not let those storms stand in your way
You have the whole universe to conquer
So, just keep the faith my son and
Start climbing

You know, there are times when you feel there is no
one around who cares
There may even be times, my son, when you think
you are the only one out there
But, all the time, there is someone, watching every step you take
Blessing you along the way
Please believe me my son when I say

There's the sky, take it, for it's your limit
The clouds are only ladders for you to climb
And the stars are lights so that you can find your way
So just keep the faith, my son, and
Start climbing

x

INTRODUCTION

I had a conversation with a colleague of mine, Rev. Dr. L.A. Gatewood of Ohio, who explained, "God's blessings are like someone putting an unlimited amount of money in a checking account just for you to spend at your discretion. But, they did not teach you how to write a check; that, my friend, is the mystery of life and the blessing waiting us all. We just need to learn how to make a proper withdrawal."

He gave another example, this one about the Beverly Hillbillies, who moved into a mansion with two rolling stairways on each side going upward to the many rooms on the second level. But the new owners thought someone else must stay up there, so they initially settled on living in the foyer. I believe many of us are like the Beverly Hillbillies. We were given a mansion but think we are limited to the foyer. Nobody told us that the whole mansion belongs to us!

During my twenty-plus years of ministering, I made some unfortunate discoveries about our churches as a whole:

1. Generally, we failed to tell our parishioners of the wonderful blessing that is all theirs.

2. Normally, we failed to show them how to tap into the resources that will allow them to enjoy these blessings.

3. Generally, we have not taught them how to write that check to withdraw from their unlimited resources.

Given these unfortunate findings, spiritual leaders must step up to the plate by providing guidance to help parishioners acquire knowledge and skills to cash in on these blessings. This book is designed to help you learn how to not only write that check but cash it by learning how to tap into the divine resources that I believe are at our disposal and within our reach.

I pray that after reading this publication, your life will be enriched to the point of not only having "life and having it more abundantly," but to the point of leading others to a better life in Christ, right here on earth which is what we should be doing as Christ's Disciples.

Mind you, this is not a get-rich-quick scheme. If that is what you are looking for, this book is not for you. But, if you are looking for more fulfillment out of your life, I believe you have come to the right place.

I heard a sermon delivered by the Reverend Donna Anderson of Illinois entitled, "What Is in Your House." Her text was taken from 2 Kings, fourth chapter, about the widow who had nothing but a small portion of oil and was faced with losing her sons to creditors. Reverend Anderson masterfully illustrated how we have blessings at our disposal but have not taken an inventory of our resources. She told a story of a fisherman who seemed to catch more fish than his colleagues but, for some odd reason, threw all fish that measured more than eight inches back into the water. When asked why, he responded that he only had an eight-inch fry pan at home.

So many of us make similar decisions in our lives, limiting our horizons while constantly praying The Prayer of Jabez, not realizing that God has already given us what we need to enlarge our territory. This book will help you take that inventory to discover the blessing that God may have already made available to you.

CLAIMING YOUR INHERITANCE

"A GATEWAY TO A RICH AND FULFILLING LIFE"

CHAPTER ONE

INSPIRATION

Be Inspired by Your Love for Life

And now I will show you the most excellent way. If I speak in the tongues of men and of angels, but have not love, I am only a resounding gong or a clanging cymbal. If I have the gift of prophecy and can fathom all mysteries and all knowledge, and if I have a faith that can move mountains, but have not love, I am nothing. If I give all I possess to the poor and surrender my body to the flames, but have not love, I gain nothing. Love is patient, love is kind. It does not envy, it does not boast, it is not proud. It is not rude, it is not self-seeking, it is not easily angered, and it keeps no record of wrongs. Love does not delight in evil but rejoices with the truth. It always protects, always trusts, always hopes, and always perseveres. Love never fails. But where there are prophecies, they will cease; where there are tongues, they will be stilled; where there is knowledge, it will pass away. For we know in part and we prophesy in part, but when perfection comes, the imperfect disappears. When I was a child, I talked like a child, I thought like a child, I reasoned like a child. When I became a man, I put childish ways behind me. Now we see but a poor reflection as in a mirror; then we shall see face to face. Now I know in part, then I shall know fully, even as I am fully known. And now these three remain; faith, hope and love. But the greatest of these is love.

1 Corinthians 13:1–13 (NIV, New International Version)

1

Ann Romney, in her attempt to convince American voters of the character of her husband as a viable candidate for the presidency, started her speech at the Republican Convention of 2012 by saying (and I paraphrase), "I want to talk to you today about *love*." Why did she start the most important speech that she probably ever made in public with love? Why would she use this term as a political tool for the highest office in the land?

Well, my friend, it's because love never fails; and if she could convince the country of his love for her and her love for him, she would have humanized a man that many people viewed as cold and unapproachable. She would have been successful in presenting him as warm, compassionate, caring, and, above all, concerned about the American people.

Michelle Obama had her turn, not only convincing her listeners about the love that resonated between her and President Obama but also a love that began with their parents' unconditional love, which inspired and empowered President Obama to make decisions that he believed best for the middle-class American, despite the opposition he faced.

I believe the greatest inspiration for living is love, and so do both women. They delivered the message in 1 Corinthians, which was an excellent approach.

On the other hand, the absence of love can be nonproductive and downright deadly. I remember reading about Adolf Hitler and the Aryan Race Philosophy of developing a superior race. They would select a certain group of women to impregnate with the sperm of a highly selected male in order to produce what they called a superior being. It was Hitler's plan to train these beings, preferably men, to take over the world and be the rulers. However, when the babies were born, many of them died off. This caused a great concern until one scientist hypothesized that the babies were dying because of a "lack of love."

It was theorized that the child was removed from its mother right after birth, which did not give the child a chance to bond or feel the connection that Homo sapiens need to survive. Unlike baby chicks and other animals, a human being must feel that initial love connection to survive.

Now, if you can accept that theory, then you will understand me further theorizing that all through life, we are in need of some form of love connection to develop that zeal for living. Some psychologists will argue that, without some form of love connection, people will ultimately lose their zeal for life, which happens to many suicide victims. Although I am not a professional counselor or psychologist, my experience leads me to strongly believe that without the presence of some form of love, the average person will eventually lose the will to live. Love is essential to life.

So, what about love? It was Tina Turner who asked the question in her hit song "What's love got to do with it?" The question needed to be asked because, in our society, we use the term so loosely that we have difficulty defining it. Ask three people to tell you what love means, and you will get three (or more) different explanations. We have a very hard time agreeing on its meaning.

Love has everything to do with it: life, success, our very existence.

In order to know and understand love and the powerful benefits it brings, we need to revisit its meaning. Let's look at its origins.

Degrees of Love

Paul recognized the Roman Christians as the "beloved of God, called to be saints" (Romans 1:7). The Greek for "beloved" is *agapetos*, which is derived from the Greek *agape*, meaning "love." Here it means "loved ones." There are four Greek words used to express love found in the New Testament. These are *èros*, *stauros*, *phileos*, and agapetos. These words are defined as follows:

ÈROS is the love between man and woman. From the Greek word èros, we get our English word "erotic." Èros is used for sensual or sexual love, which, if used in the right context, contains nothing sinful. The sensual love between husband and wife is part of a good Christian marriage, but by no means the only type of love that should be present for a healthy relationship. Many great novels, plays, and movies have depicted èros. One example is *Dr. Zhivago*, the story of an accomplished physician of aristocratic status who risked everything to be with his common lover. Others were Shakespeare's *Romeo and Juliet* and history's Cleopatra and Mark Antony. The greatest example to me was my grandparents Paul and Louise. They were married for more than seventy years and loved so deeply that when my grandmother made her earthly transition, Grandpa willingly followed within a nine-month period. Like most of these love stories, there's a side effect. In most cases, life is not worth living when that precious love is taken away.

STAUROS/STORGE is a love shared between family members. You could be said to have storge toward your mother, father, and other family members. This love comes natural but can be altered or minimized due to traumatic experience, unfavorable parenting, or very negative relationships. Dysfunctional or abusive parenting is not the norm but may occur when persons become parents prematurely or without comprehending and accepting the responsibility of Christian parenting. Man and woman should also have a storge love toward one another. It is that natural love that evolves with time, familiarity, and the experiences of love through a relationship that is healthy and supportive. Children are known to elevate storge and, with time, enhance this precious benefit of procreation, which is designed by God.

Although I have read some wonderful stories of orphans who have triumphed over many adversities to become happy and successful, those stories are few. Storge has fueled so many great outcomes. I am convinced that the love of family is so powerful it kindles life's zeal.

PHILEOS is love expressed between friends. In a sense, phileos is a selfish type of love. It is expressed when two people see something that they like or can relate to in each other. In other words, I will not phileos you unless something in your nature or character appeals to my nature or character. Phileos can also be expressed through our love of humankind. Phileos is the element that causes us to send that care package overseas or donate to the Feed the Children campaign. Phileos is that brotherly and sisterly love that sometimes even transcends race, color, creed, religion, ethnic origin, gender, class, economical status, and even languages. You know, that good old brotherly love.

AGAPE is the scriptural ideal for love. When we think of love, we always attach a connotation of emotion—such as a "warm, loving feeling"—toward another person. Agape, in direct contrast to the English word "love," has no connotation of emotion attached to it. The other three Greek words for love—èros, phileos, and storge—all have emotional connotations or condition. I do not mean to imply that agape cannot be accompanied by emotion, although it is plainly stated scripturally that agape can function equally well with or without emotion. Agape can be defined as "seeking to do the highest good for the other party, with total disregard for self, condition, or the other person's response." That is to say: "I'm willing to die for your love!" God's love for man and to man is always expressed as agape and never as phileos, èros, or storge.

This type of love is probably the hardest for humanity to assimilate because we are emotional beings. It is human for us to always rely on an emotional cause or source of our love. But agape takes us beyond that period. You see, all the other forms of love—phileos, storge, èros—are conditional loves. These types of love depend on how others respond and feed our love. But, Christ called us to go beyond the point of emotion or condition, where we feel an investment or reciprocating exchange or obligation. Christ challenges us to tap into another source that compels us to give and respond unconditionally: to love, just because the Christ in me loves the Christ in you. This is a divine love, a redemptive love because you are a child of God, a fellow human being that is in need of forgiveness, acceptance and redemption. I love you because, well, just because. I really have no explanation for it, it's just there.

We need all four types of love to ensure a successful and fulfilling life. We need phileos to feel valued, wanted, and accepted. We need storge to feel connected and supported, like we get and should receive from family. We strive for èros to make us feel bonded and affectionately around and attracted to another human being of the opposite sex, just to put a little spice in our lives. And finally, we need agape, that redeeming and unconditional love that only comes from God through Christ and through us. The love that will forgive us and allow us to carry on, even in our darkest hours when we feel a failure and undeserving of God's love.

I believe, beloved that we need to experience all four types of love. Although all love is an extension from God, as humans, we need to experience these loves from each other as well.

I remember meeting a young lady who appeared to have all she needed for a successful life at a homeless program. She was an edu-cated, experienced nurse but lacked those four types of love from her family. She was lacking in the most powerful source of acceptance and value. Life has many crooks and turns, and we may go through a series of changes, but in each and every stage that life takes us through, we need to use one of these loves to keep us together and weather the storm.

Because this nurse could not receive storge, she had no other choice but to search for other types of love to sustain her. She over emphasized èros, which became the guiding force, or pathway she took to get the storge, phileos, and agape for which she searched and longed. She found it in a homeless man, who had nothing, wanted nothing, and was capable of giving nothing but èros. As tragic as it may seem to us, this love satisfied her, at least on the surface. It was better than the so-called love she experienced at home. All of us crave for love in all four of its stages. Without these, we find ourselves making some weird and unclear choices to fill the void. I think it was Dolly Parton who sang, "Looking for love in all the wrong places." People will fill the void with any one of these types of loves if one is missing.

Again, our Savior, Jesus the Christ, gave us the key:

The most important one, answered Jesus, is this: Hear, O Israel, the LORD our God, the LORD is one. Love the LORD your God with all your heart and with all your soul and with all your mind and with all your strength. The second is this: Love your neighbor as yourself. There is no commandment greater than these.

Mark 12:29–31

God is calling and expecting us to do more than love him. We must love and demonstrate that love through the people with whom we come into contact. We must show and exemplify the greatest commandment of God.

As the Father has loved me, so have I loved you. Now remain in my love. If you obey my commandments, you will remain in my love, just as I have obeyed my Father's commands and remain in his love. I have told you this so that my joy may be in you and your joy may be complete. My command is this: Love each other as I have loved you. Greater love has no one than this, that he lay down his life for his friends.

John 15:9–13

Does this mean you are your brother's keeper? Yes, read further, and think about your decisions. That is exactly what Christ means. How can we love the Lord, say we are Christians, and have the love of Christ in us but walk past our brother or sister in the street and not even think of helping? Some of us even have the nerve to voice frustration at having to see them, let alone having to refuse helping them. Not because we feel threatened or lack the resources to help them but, rather, we just don't care. Now if you have other reasons, other legitimate reasons for not helping, then this piece is not for you. If you fall into the first category, then beloved, please remember the parable of the Good Samaritan:

But he wanted to justify himself, so he asked Jesus, "And who is my neighbor?" In reply Jesus said: "A man was going down from Jerusalem to Jericho, when he fell into the hands of robbers. They stripped him of his clothes, beat him and went away, leaving him half dead. A priest happened to be going down the same road, and when he saw the man, he

7

passed by on the other side. So too, a Levite, when he came to the place and saw him, passed by on the other side. But a Samaritan, as he traveled, came where the man was and when he saw him, he took pity on him.

He went to him and bandaged his wounds, pouring on oil and wine. Then he put the man on his own donkey, took him to an inn and took care of him. The next day he took out two silver coins and gave them to the innkeeper. "Look after him," he said, "and when I return, I will reimburse you for any extra expense you may have."

Luke 10:29–35

You may notice and remember this passage of scripture where Christ explained the law of love—that you must love God with all your heart, mind, soul, and strength but also love your neighbor as yourself. But the expert on the law, Christ, wanted to justify himself. You know what that means, beloved.

Like us, sometimes he wanted to justify his attitude toward other people and why he did not love them as he should have. But Jesus told the parable of the Good Samaritan, showing that we don't have a choice when the opportunity arises to help people. Everyone is our brother and sister, children of God, and we cannot justify our reason for helping some and refusing to help others.

We must demonstrate total devotion to God and to loving your neighbor as you love yourself. But, you ask, "Who is our neighbor? Is It not the people next door or the ones in our neighborhood?" No, it's the world, wherever we find living beings. It does not matter our unique differences, for we all have one commonality: we are the children of God.

In the parable of the Good Samaritan, Jesus shows agape in its purest sense. Here was a man who had no reason to stop and help one who appeared to represent the lost and downtrodden that we often reject. Yet, the Samaritan was moved beyond racial and ethnic boundaries to show love, care, and compassion.

Loving somebody who loves us back is easy, good, and commendable. When we love and care for someone for whom we normally have no reason to care, that caring or love is divine. This is where God is eager to shine through us if we would just let him in. This light is in us already, just waiting to burst forth if we let love abide in us. Watch little children of ages two, three, and four before they learn our demonic system of prejudice and bigotry; they will show you how to love the agape way.

I remember hearing a story of a rich man who decided to have lunch at the downtown café after concluding a meeting with his banker on a business deal. While he was eating lunch, he noticed what appeared to be a woman just standing at the corner. It was quite cold outside, so her standing there as long as he was eating his meal got his attention. After leaving the café, he approached the corner, only to find out that she was a bag lady begging. He gave her a dollar and went on his way.

Later that evening, as his butler served his dinner, his mind went back to that poor lady standing on the corner, begging. His thoughts began to haunt him, and he grew disturbed. That night, he could not sleep; he kept thinking about that poor woman. As he finally dozed off to sleep, he dreamed that he was face to face with God. He asked God why, if he loved everyone enough to send the Christ, he did not care for that bag lady on the corner.

God responded to him by saying, *"Yes, my son, I do care, that's why I sent you there!"*

I believe many of us can be of so much help to the poor that we can wipe out poverty in this country and perhaps the entire world. But because of our greed and selfishness, the poor will always be with us. Now, that is not a reason for us to give up hope, rather it is the divine purpose of the believers to show the way—no matter how hard, how helpless, or how difficult it may seem. God created humanity for HER glory; it is through God, working in the affairs of humankind that makes all the difference in the world. But, make no mistake about it, the work is not just for the wealthy, but we who may appear to have little can do the most work. Little by little, you can make the difference.

But, the greatest of these is LOVE.

CLAIMING YOUR
INHERITANCE

"A GATEWAY TO A RICH AND FULFILLING LIFE"

CHAPTER TWO

NIA

You Are Here for a Purpose

*So God created man in HIS own image, in the image of God, HE cre-
ated him; male and female, HE created them. God blessed them and
said to them, "Be fruitful and increase in number; fill the earth and
subdue it. Rule over the fish of the sea and the birds of the air and over
every living creature that moves on the ground."*

Genesis 1:27–28

Regardless of how you believe humankind came into being, we
need to agree that it was for a reason. To think that it was just the result
of a Big Bang or a chemical explosion that coincidentally formed human
life will not allow you to utilize the gifts I am introducing, nor will you
believe that there is an inheritance to be claimed.

Although I do not believe it was as simple as God scooping a hunk
of clay from the ground and forming a human being, I believe God's infinite wisdom and knowledge planned and executed the creation of the
cosmos with each and every molecule in place to bring us to this point
in our existence. There was no Big Bang or chemical explosion or imbalance—no war of the cosmos—but a plan and execution under a divine
order. And you were a part of that divine order. It is not by accident that
we are here and, for the most part, all with hearts, livers, kidneys, and
other parts of our bodies working in sync with each other. And, it is not

by accident that we can reproduce children who have combined features, body movement, and actually have our mannerisms with little effort.

Yes, beloved, I believe we are not a result of a space accident, mistake, fluke of the cosmos, or a mishap of atomic molecules colliding in bionomical forces. I believe the earth is the result of God's deliberate, omnipotent plan, and you are part of the plan, whether you like it or not, accept it or not, believe it or not, live by it or not, and conceive it or not.

You Are It.

What is meant by "in HIS image?" Merriam-Webster defines image as, "A reproduction or imitation or a formed representation of a person or thing." It is further defined as "an imitation in solid form." To me, the latter definition could mean early form. The definition continues with "exact likeness"—Wow! Do you know what that is telling me? We all have the capability of taking on the likeness of God. As one continues to explore the definition, we see the definition "a tangible or visible representation." Now this is the most significant and impressive meaning of all. It suggests that we are made in God's image to be an earthly, tangible, and visible representation of God. I believe that's exactly what Christ was saying to Thomas and Phillip in John 14:

If you really knew me, you would know my Father as well. From now on, you do know him and have seen him. Then Philip said, "Lord show us the Father and that will be enough for us."
Now, what Christ said afterward is the key...

Jesus answered: Don't you know me, Philip, even after I have been among you such a long time? Anyone who has seen me has seen the father. How can you say, "Show us the Father?" Don't you believe that I am in the Father and that the Father is in me? The words I say to you are not just my own. Rather, it is the Father, living in me, who is doing his work. Believe me when I say that I am in the Father and the Father is in me, or at least believe on the evidence of the miracles themselves.

Verses 9–11

Then he gave us a bomb of theological thought.

I tell you the truth, anyone who has faith in me will do what I have been doing. He will do even greater things than these, because I am going to the Father. And I will do whatever you ask in my name, so that the Son may bring glory to the Father. You may ask me for anything in my name and I will do it. If you love me, you will obey what I command. And I will ask the Father and he will give you another Counselor to be with you forever.

Verses 12–16

Wow! This is great news, my brothers and sisters. This passage of scripture introduces to us the concept of the Trinity and confirms what is talked about in the creation: the Father, the Son, and the Holy Spirit. And with the three of them working within us, we can do all things; not just for empowerment or performance but to represent God here on earth, in everything we do and say.

This scripture also points out the purpose of us being on earth. *We are to do the work of the Father* and glorify him through our works. We are not just to repeat what Jesus the Christ did during his earthly journey, but we are to go beyond that point and do more. Yes, that means healing the sick through heart surgery; curing cancer and eliminating viruses; giving sight to the physically, mentally, and emotionally blind; and much, much more than you or I can imagine.

Doing the work of the Father also means bringing hope and deliverance to this struggling and, in some cases, quite sinful world through love and compassion for all humankind. This can be accomplished in so many ways by so many people, and that, my friend, is why you and I are here.

This is the reason you are on earth, and this is the reason why you are unique and as special as you are. God has sent you to earth as a spirit. SHE blew your spirit into a body, which then became a living soul, to do great things in representation of the Creator throughout our earthly journey that we call life.

This is not a task that is achieved by Jesus the Christ alone or by noteworthy persons in our history. This is a charge that God has given you and I, all of us, no matter how small or large the task. This, my friend, is where the key word *stewardship* enters. Stewardship is what we do with the life that God has given to us. To be a steward is to care for something for which we have been entrusted. God has entrusted us with life, an earthly journey, and a divine task. What are you going to do with it? What if I tell you that you can do a lot? But, many of us fail; not because of our lack of ability but because we fail to recognize and perfect the tools and resources that God has given us to carry out our task.

In what areas of our lives is stewardship demonstrated? In the following pages, I will share with you the acts and steps involved in stewardship that will enable all of us to obtain all that God has for us. It will enable us to claim our heavenly and divine inheritance and become the rich heir of the throne, possessing all the riches of God and living a full, happy, and rewarding life here on earth.

> "Notice, I am not talking about:
> A pie in the sky
> And the sweet by and by;
> Or getting your rewards
> After you die"

Christ said, "I have come that you may have life, and have it to the full."

John 10:10b

But we first need to understand that God, our Creator, has a purpose for each of our lives. Jehovah did not just blow breath into your body for nothing. I believe, with all my heart, that Elohim created you for a specific purpose. The acknowledgement, development, planning, and execution of that purpose are up to you.

You may notice that I sometimes refer to God by the different names used by different tongues: "Jehovah (English), Elohim (Hebrew), and Yahweh. I may even slip from time to time and refer to God in the second person as HE or SHE. Not that I am being disrespectful, but I just want to remind you that if Jehovah can be a HE, then maybe Yahweh can be a SHE. Why? Because I believe God is a spirit and has no place or need for gender reference. Further, that Spirit God, that Spirit the Creator, has made you and is willing to empower you to do great things.

But you will receive power when the Holy Spirit comes on you, and you will be my witness in Jerusalem, and in all Judea and Samaria, and to the ends of the earth.

Acts 1:8

What if I tell you that you are to be a witness for the LORD, not only in your home but also in your neighborhood, city, country, and the world? But what are you to witness? Well, to witness is to bring forth evidence. "Evidence of what?" you may ask. Evidence of how good God is. Well, yes, that's right, but how can you show evidence of how good God is without experiencing what you are to show or share as evidence? Your witnessing has to be more than just words.

We can preach to a person until we are blue in the face, but until they can see evidence they can relate to, it may not be as effective.

I remember hearing a Boy Scout speech that really stuck with me. The scout said, "I would rather see a sermon any day, than to hear one." I did not interpret that statement to mean the scout did not like sermons; rather it was more effective and relevant when he could see the meaning of the sermon in action. If you agree, then more people than only preachers should be preaching. We all are ministers in this respect. We all have the capability and responsibility of sharing a divine message with others by what we show and display to them in our everyday living. This is being a witness for the LORD. Witnessing is far more than verbally preaching to others.

So I say, live by the Spirit, and you will not gratify the desires of the sinful nature. For the sinful nature desires what is contrary to the Spirit, and the Spirit what is contrary to the sinful nature. They are in conflict with each other so that you do not do what you want. But if you are led by the Spirit, you are not under the law. The acts of the sinful nature are obvious: sexual immorality, impurity and debauchery, idolatry and witchcraft, hatred, discord, jealousy, fits of rage, selfish ambition, dissensions, factions and envy; drunkenness, orgies, and the like. I warn you, as I did before, that those who live like this will not inherit the kingdom of God.

But the fruit of the Spirit is love, joy, peace, patience, kindness, goodness, faithfulness, gentleness, and self-control. Against such things there is no law. Those who belong to Christ Jesus have crucified the sinful nature with its passions and desires. Since we live by the Spirit, let us keep in step with the Spirit. Let us not become conceited, the provoking of envying of each other.

Galatians 5:16–25

There's a poem that I picked up some time ago called "I Have Two Natures," which I believe fits very nicely here:

I have two natures on my breast
One is foul, one is blessed
One I love, and the other I hate
But the one I feed will dominate
Author Unknown

Your best witness tool is for people to see the Christ in you. When you exhibit the fruits of the Spirit in your everyday life, people will take notice.

I often speak to people who want to know how to start witnessing to people. They ask, "What do I say to them, especially those of other beliefs or who do not believe at all—you know, like the Muslims,

16

Buddhists, or even Atheists?" Well, if you walk in the Spirit, you are actually witnessing to all before you even speak. You are showing the gifts of the Spirit that cannot be denied by the eyes. Then you speak to them; but, please, don't be on the attack.

Whether you agree with another's belief or not, remember, tearing down another's ideas does not result in reception. No one feels receptive when being attacked. Instead of telling them where and how they are wrong, take another approach. Show the person how they are better off adopting your lifestyle. Remember, you do that by first showing the Fruits of the Spirit.

The Reverend Jonathan D. Dames said, "Yes, He [Jehovah], calls and appeals to each of us: 'Whom shall I send and who will go for us?'" in his book *The Church Member's Guide*.

My friend, you are the answer to that call. You are needed to help win souls to Christ. Just as others have been helpful in winning you to Christ, you must be helpful in winning others. The first thing that Andrew did after he accepted the call to discipleship was to go and find his brother Peter. It is the parting commission of Christ to His disciples in Matthew 28:16–20…

Then the eleven disciples went to Galilee, to the mountain where Jesus had told them to go. When they saw him, they worshiped him; but some doubted. Then Jesus came to them and said, "All authority in heaven and on earth has been given to me. Therefore go and make disciples of all nations, baptizing them in the name of the Father and of the Son and of the Holy Spirit, and teaching them to obey everything I have commanded you. And surely I am with you always, to the very end of the age.

How do we witness and attract others through our accomplishments and achievements? Well, as good stewards, we can show others God's blessings and glory by example. One small example may be by driving a new or recently purchased car. Now, before you go off on me about materialism, an automobile is pretty close to a necessity in this country of ours. But, it needs to represent not just a blessing but also

17

good stewardship. Using an automobile, for instance, can determine what type of message you are conveying. Driving a twenty-year-old clunker will give a different message than a new car. Using the same example, driving a modest American-made vehicle will give a different message than a foreign luxury car. Subcompact versus a limousine is also props that can convey different messages for our witnessing.

We can extend our examples by using homes, clothes, or any items that we own to show God's blessings, along with our good stewardship and modest living. When we witness, we display God's mercy and grace upon our lives. My friend, God's mercy and grace can only be demonstrated with a good living example: health, prosperity, comfort, peace, balance, and satisfaction. We cannot witness to anyone about the goodness of the LORD by displaying a less than glorified and grateful life.

Let's take another approach to recruiting for the household of faith. Picture yourself as a salesperson for Christ. Have you ever gone window shopping, not really looking for anything particular and not really in need of anything specific, and been approached by a salesperson who convinced you that you would be better off with that watch or piece of jewelry they presented to you? They did not start their sales pitch with an insult or by showing you how tacky you looked. Rather, they presented that item as something that would enhance your looks or appearance. Such is the case with evangelizing or giving witness. You will attract more people by showing them, through your display of the spirit, how their life can be enhanced by accepting the Christ as their Lord and Savior.

You are the salt of the earth. But if the salt loses its saltiness, how can it be made salty again? It is no longer good for anything, except to be thrown out and trampled by men.

Matthew 5:13

You may say, "Wait a minute, sir, you are supposed to tell me how to claim my inheritance, and so far you have been telling me of my responsibility to God through stewardship and, now, witnessing."

Well, my friend, in order to have an inheritance, you need to belong to a family of wealth, right? So, I need you to know your family has all the types of wealth and security that you need, and it is yours for the claiming. But, how would anyone know unless you can show that you are a member of the family? Just like any family, you need to have a particular identity, DNA, characteristic, make-up, and family feature. So, you need to know how to think, act, and operate like a member of the royal family.

The Bible provides instructions in the scriptures that tell us how we are to carry ourselves as members of this great family. One of the ways we can identify with the family is to know and exemplify who you are: the Salt of the Earth. Like salt, you are a preservative, a keeper, someone who keeps things fresh and healthy, spiritually. Like salt, you bring flavor, seasoning, and accentuation into the lives of others. In other words, put a little pizzazz in your ministry and a little zip in your step as you go about ministering to others.

When people see you coming, they should think, "Wow! If this is what Christianity is all about, then I want it. I long for the brightness, the flavor, the zeal, the excitement of showing the grace and mercy of God in the lives of HIS people." You are the salesperson; you are the recruiter; for you are the only Christ someone may see. Therefore, in you they should see love, forgiveness, mercy, grace, compassion, and, above all, redemption. In displaying Christ in your everyday life, someone may ask you, "What can I do to have a life like yours? What must I do to be saved, to be a part of this wonderful family, to be counted as one of God's kingdom kids?" Now, here is the bonus:

"TO INHERIT, YOU MUST RECRUIT."

And the more you recruit, the more inheritance will come your way, and the richer your life will become. But, if we hide our identity, we will lose our flavor, our saltiness, and, like the One-Talent Servant who buried his talent, we will become good for nothing—to be thrown out and trampled by men. God forbid! Let your light shine, continue to flavor the earth by your witnessing of God and love and grace. Let the world know who you are—God's child, a kingdom kid—and identify that you are one of the heirs of the throne.

Let's take another look at our witnessing.

After this the Lord appointed seventy-two others and sent them two by two ahead of him to every town and place where he was about to go. He told them, "The harvest is plentiful, but the workers are few. Ask the LORD of the harvest, therefore, to send out workers into his harvest field. Go! I am sending you out like lambs among wolves. Do not take a purse or bag or sandals, and do not greet anyone on the road. When you enter a house, first say: 'Peace to this house.' If a man of peace is there, your peace will rest on him; if not, it will return to you. Stay in the house, eating and drinking whatever they give you, for the worker deserves his wages. Do not move around from house to house."

Luke 10:1–7

Like many families, you have an obligation to keep up the family name and identity, and what you do or do not do can bring shame or disgrace to the reputation that others before you accomplished. As a steward in God's family, we also have an obligation to be faithful in carrying out the mission and objectives of the family, which are dictated by the Holy Spirit. As a kid, I was trained and designated certain duties as my contribution to the family. Through my training, my parents instilled in us how important it was to represent the family well and to work hard in upholding the family name. At home, however, there were certain chores that I was responsible for, especially when our father died and our mother found herself in the position of rearing six children by herself. It was rough for us, but we were taught to be faithful and diligent in upholding our family values. If needed, we were to take charge in defense of the family name by displaying the characteristics taught by our parents.

All authority in heaven and on earth has been given to me. Therefore go and make disciples of all nations, baptizing them in the name of the

Father and of the Son and of the Holy Spirit, and teaching them to obey everything I have commanded you. And surely I am with you always, to the very end of the age.

Matthew 28:18–20

Christ was sending the eleven and others out into the world to be his witnesses. By doing so, many lives would be changed, saved, and improved through their teachings. Christianity was never meant to be kept within for oneself. Christianity was and is meant to be shared and spread throughout the world. You probably have heard many preachers refer to Matthew 28:18–20 as the Great Commission, for it is when he charged his disciples with spreading the Gospel throughout the world. But, I believe they were to offer more than salvation, more than baptism; for it was a complete way of life. As a matter of fact, some theologians will tell you that the Christian movement was first called the Way Movement. The disciples had been introduced to a new way of living. They thought differently, walked differently, and their entire life was different.

Just as the disciples were inducted into the household of faith, we are expected to change to a new life and a new way of living. This life change was not just to baptize folk and then go home until the next Sunday. Oh no, instead, one is inducted into a totally different way of life, a life of total wealth. Yes, just as the disciples were rich, we are the rich people—not in money but in resources, spiritual gifts, graces, and power.

I believe we can have a similar life, even right here in the United States of America, but we must undergo a change. We must first take our blinders off and see clearly. Most of us are blind in thinking earthly substance is our means of wealth.

Money, assets, and holdings define us in America, but that is not the way God sees us. God wants us to have something far more valuable than money or possessions. God wants us to have the same gifts that the Christ possessed on earth, which were not obtained by earthly means. Yes, my friend, God wants us to live a life that is independent of earthly means or circumstances. I believe God is ready to empower us, just as he empowered Christ and the disciples to heal the sick, cast our demons, and, yes, even walk on water. If we have powers like that, money will become far less important. So you want to be rich? Tap into the power source that will enable you to do things that money cannot provide—power that will make you a spiritual reservoir for others. By being God's witness, Jehovah has given us authority to take charge, as the Great Commission indicates.

In his book *Spiritual Authority*, Watchman Nee stated, "What a risk God has taken in instituting authorities! What a loss God will incur if the delegated authorities HE institutes misrepresent HIM!"

But there is also danger in misrepresentation. Remember the passage about the Jews who attempted to use the authority of God by speaking the name of Jesus:

Some Jews who went around driving out evil spirits tried to invoke the name of the Lord Jesus over those who were demon possessed. They would say, "In the name of Jesus, whom Paul preaches, I command you to come out." Seven sons of Sceva, a Jewish chief priest, were doing this. One day the evil spirit answered them, "Jesus I know, and I know Paul, but who are you?" Then the man who has the evil spirit jumped on them and overpowered them all. He gave them such a beating that they ran out of the house naked and bleeding.

Acts 19:13–16

So, you can't just speak authority, you must know it and earn it. God himself must delegate HER authority to you. Willingness to be a witness for God opens the delegated authority that comes from God; and no one, not even demons, can take that authority and power away. So, be a witness and obtain all that you need for an empowered and enriched life, not for the riches' sake or the power's sake but because you love the LORD and acknowledge that you are being called according to God's purpose and will.

Witnessing is designed to bring on a change in others, to offer them a better life. You can't offer something that you don't have yourself, so I believe the moment you surrender to God and obey HIS will in your life, God will give you something will open the eyes of others that so that they too can see the benefits in being a Child of God.

My younger brother sent me a CD from Oklahoma and on the CD was the sermon of an unknown preacher. The sermon was so powerful to him that he wanted to share it with me. The preacher shared a story about a young man who had just completed college and returned to his home-town to begin his career as a professional. With his degree in his hand one morning, he announced that he was going downtown to the bank to take out a loan for a car. His father, who had made it to the third grade in school, was so proud of his son that he offered to co-sign for his loan.

"No, Dad, I don't need you now, I have my degree," the young man resisted.

"Are you sure you don't want me to at least go with you, son? I know the people at the bank who can help you."

"No, Pops, I got my degree, I can handle it," the young man insisted.

The young man entered the bank and sat in the loan department lounge until a seasoned gentleman asked if he could help him.

"Yes, sir, I came to get an auto loan," the young man responded.

"Very well, what are you using for collateral?" the gentleman asked.

"Co-what?" the young man said.

"Collateral; what kind of backing can we use to assure the loan?"

"Oh." The young man smiled. "I have my degree."

The loan officer smiled and said, "Well, son, I'm happy for you, and I know it will serve you well in the future. As for now, however, we must turn you down on your auto loan."

Just as the young man was about to turn and leave the bank, he heard a familiar voice saying, "Excuse me."

"How are you, sir?"

"Dad! What are you doing here? I told you that I didn't need you. The bank has already turned me down. What could you possibly do anyway? After all, you can barely make an X."

The loan officer overheard the conversation the young man was having with his father. "Excuse me, young man, but is this your father you are talking to? Let me tell you about that X that he can barely make. It was that X that bought the farm that he worked to feed you and your seven siblings. It was that X that put clothes on your back, and that X that sent you to college to get that degree. And, whether you realize it or not, it's going to take that X to get the auto loan you need."

I shared that story, not because of the young man's ignorance or the father's love and mercy, but because it was the witnessing of that loan officer that opened the young man's eyes to see the blessings that were in his life because of a loving father.

As a witness for Jehovah, you need to tell somebody of the goodness of our Heavenly Father. Elohim has all that we need for a great and rich life. The more we tell it, the more we will be blessed with riches from on high. Oh, not by dollars and cents, but in so many other ways that your Blessings Cup may just overflow. Being a witness is like being a salesperson for God. The more you sell or lead a person to conversion, the more commission you get. What is a heavenly commission but lots of stuff far more valuable than silver or gold and full of bonuses that keep coming as we keep witnessing. And as our converts mature and become witnesses themselves, we receive even more. Like that loan officer; not only did he help the young man see his blessings, he gained a new customer, one who has the potential to do a lot of business with the bank for years to come. After all, *he's got his degree.*

Witnessing also comes with power. The power that comes from God by way of the Holy Spirit:

Again Jesus said, "Peace be with you! As the Father has sent me, I am sending you." And with that he breathed on them and said, "Receive the Holy Spirit. If you forgive anyone his sins, they are forgiven; if you do not forgive them, they are not forgiven.

John 20:21–23

24

To be a witness also means to have power; power to carry out the will of God in our lives. This power comes from the Holy Spirit, the same Spirit that Jesus had, the same Holy Spirit that Christ gave to his disciples, and the same Holy Spirit that overcame the disciples on the day of Pentecost. And it is the same Holy Spirit that will empower us to be a witness and keep us connected to the vine.

You know the story of the "True Vine."

I am the true vine, and my Father is the gardener. He cuts off every branch in me that bears no fruit, while every branch that does bear fruit he prunes so that it will be even more fruitful. You are already clean because of the word I have spoken to you. Remain in me, and I will remain in you. No branch can bear fruit by itself; it must remain in the vine. Neither can you bear fruit unless you remain in me.

I am the vine, you are the branches. If a man remains in me and I in him, he will bear much fruit; apart from me you can do nothing. If anyone does not remain in me, he is like a branch that is thrown away and withers; such branches are picked up, thrown into the fire and burned. If you remain in me and my words remain in you, ask whatever you wish, and it will be given you. This is to my Father's glory, that you bear much fruit, showing yourselves to be my disciples.

Gospel of St. John 15:1–8

It is clear that authority and power come from being connected. And, as Nee points out, you must be in the line of authority that comes from God, to Christ, and then to His disciples to witness to others and the world. That's you, my friend. You are the one to give witness to God's word, power, love, mercy, grace, and, most of all, forgiveness. But in doing so, you cannot use lip service. Like the Boy Scout who would rather see a sermon than hear one, most of us are visual. Showing an example on how to live, how to communicate with others, and, yes, how to forgive may be the best opportunity for you to give witness. The passages from the Book of John tell us that witnessing brings forth power and growth, because even the branch that is producing is pruned so that it can bear more fruit.

I need to share with you a story of a young man who had just received a pink slip from his boss. Times were hard, and the company had to lay off workers.

On his way home, with tears in his eyes, he pondered how he would make it with his wife pregnant with their third child and being already behind in rent. As he drove down the road, he noticed what appeared to be a very expensive luxury car on the side of the road with an elderly woman standing outside. He enviously thought to himself how some people have it made, their riches can do it all for them, and they know neither need nor want. But, as he passed her, his heart changed, and he made a U-turn to see what the problem was. She, of course, was very nervous to receive his help, but she had no choice. Her driver was on vacation, and because her family had forbidden her to drive because of her age, she was unaware of the road-service procedures.

Well, the brother could see that she only needed a tire change, so he offered to change her tire. She reluctantly accepted. As he was changing the tire, the young man shared his misfortune and how his wife was expecting any week now. After he finished the tire change, the woman offered to give him money; after all, he really could have used it. But, surprisingly, the young man refused, saying he believed God would bless him if he continued to be a blessing for others. He did not accept the money. The woman could not understand it, especially with the story she heard, but she thanked him and went on her way.

Later that day, she became hungry and stopped in a diner where a sweet but very pregnant waitress took her order. While waiting on the table, they began to talk, and the elder woman realized it was the wife of the very man who helped her earlier. After eating her meal, she abruptly left the restaurant. When the waitress returned to the table, she was horrified to find the woman's seat empty. The owner would certainly take the cost of the customer's meal out of her pay.

But, as she was cleaning the table, she found five, one hundred–dollar bills wrapped in a napkin. When she arrived home, her husband shared with his wife the disappointing news. In an effort to cheer him up, she shared her story with him and showed him the five hundred dollars that would make them current on the rent. He realized it was the same woman he had helped on the road. As they were glorifying God, the phone rang, and it was his plant manager. That elder woman was the plant manager's mother. She had shared her experience with her son, who vowed to find a way to keep the young man on payroll. In the end, the young man was told to report to work the next day.

Now, our brother who stopped to help the elderly woman on the road had reasoned not to stop to help that rich person, but his heart moved him to do so, knowing that even rich folk need a blessing from God through HIS servants. He used that opportunity to witness to her. This not only impressed her, but I believe it was a pruning moment for him. You see, he could have very easily kept driving, participating in his self-pity party, but instead, he reached beyond his own emotional pain to witness to another, even one whom you would not expect him to help, just as the Good Samaritan had done. His actions did more for her than any sermon she may have heard. The story also conveys to us that witnessing is not always easy, nor does the opportunity to witness always come at an ideal time when we are ready to witness. Sometimes a person needs to witness your struggle and pain, as well as your victory and triumph, for your witnessing to be effective.

You may ask, "How can I get to the place where I can witness beyond my own pain and struggle? How can I have the power to show God's love, grace, and mercy to others when I am down and out or just ill equipped?"

Remember the disciples asked the Christ a similar question...

When they came to the crowd, a man approached Jesus and knelt before him. "Lord, have mercy on my son," he said. "He has seizures and is suffering greatly. He often falls into the fire or into the water. I brought him to your disciples, but they could not heal him."

"O unbelieving and perverse generation," Jesus replied, "how long shall I stay with you? How long shall I put up with you? Bring the boy

*here to me." Jesus rebuked the demon, and it came out of the boy, and
he was healed from that moment. Then the disciples came to Jesus in
private and asked, "Why couldn't we drive it out?" He replied, "Because
you have little faith, I tell you the truth, if you have faith as small as a
mustard seed, you can say to this mountain, 'Move from here to there'
and it will move. Nothing will be impossible for you."*

Matthew 17:14–20 (NIV)

"Howbeit this kind goeth not out but by prayer and fasting."

Matthew 17:21 (KJV, King James Version)

Yes, it may take a little work on our part. God doesn't just distribute
the power of the Holy Spirit to anyone; especially baby Christians who
may not know what to do with it or how to use it. With prayer and fasting,
we become more in tune with God and HER will in our lives. Our level of
discernment increases, as do self-discipline and direction. As witnesses
connected with the vine, we begin to see clearer who we are, in whom
we believe, and whom we serve. Through prayer and fasting, the influ-
ences of this world begin to diminish. The more we pray and fast, the less
influence the world has on us and the more spiritual power we obtain.

The more we fast and pray, the more we can overcome our obstacles and do our Master's will.

My two sisters experienced a very tragic event in their lives. Not
long ago, both of their sons departed from this life due to illness. The
entire family was devastated. Around the same time, my cousin in
another state got word that her ex-husband had died. I was surprised
to hear that one of my sisters, who had just buried her son, called and
ministered to that cousin. In the middle of their telephone conversation, the cousin, who must have been surprised herself, asked my sister,
"Didn't you just bury your son? How is it that you are calling to comfort
me? After all, he was my *ex*-husband." My sister answered by acknowledging that a divorce decree cannot erase that which is in the heart,

nor can we ignore the need to comfort others, even when we ourselves are in pain.

One of my favorite poems is "Footprints" (circa 1871–1880), in which a man dreamed that he was looking over his life as he journeyed along the seashore. He noticed that during the highlights of his life, when things were going well, there were two sets of footprints along the shore. But, at the low points of his life, when things were tough and painful for him, he only saw one set of footprints. He questioned God as to why, when things were going right, there were two sets of footprints but during the hard times he only saw one set of footprints. "My dear child," the LORD responded, "I would never leave or forsake you even during the bad times, for it was at those times that I carried you."

As I mentioned before, witnessing is not easy. It requires us to always be ready to do God's will at a moment's notice (or inspiration).

We need to already be connected to the very source that gives us strength, direction, inspiration, power, and discipline to do what we need to do.

Notice, this is not always verbal. Many of us have been taught that witnessing is talking—telling people about the goodness of the LORD. Although this is true, I pray that I have shared with you the old Boy Scout approach to witness: "They will know we are his witnesses by what they see in us and the work that we do."

Notice, beloved, I did not include Faith. Why? Because faith does not come from God, Faith comes from us. That is one of the reasons Jesus became irritated with his disciples in Matthew 17:14–21; they lacked the faith to do what Christ expected them to do. Let us not disappoint Christ or God. Let us continue to pray and fast—continue to be connected so that we can witness for our Creator the way our Lord and Savior did.

All this is from God, who reconciled us to himself through Christ and gave us the ministry of reconciliation: that God was reconciling the world to himself in Christ, not counting men's sins against them. And he has committed to us the message of reconciliation. We are therefore Christ's ambassadors, as though God were making his appeal through us. We implore you on Christ's behalf: Be reconciled to God.

2 Corinthians 5:18–20

That's right, beloved, we are called to be ambassadors for Christ, to reconcile the world to God, just as Christ reconciled you to God. So, get to work, for "you may be the only Christ a person may see." Therefore, you represent their hope, you represent their salvation, and you represent their reconciliation to God.

In order for the world to have any hope, you—yes, you—must do your part in its reconciliation. If you just sit at home and expect someone else to do the work of the Lord, it may not get done, because each and every one of us was called to do a part.

The Reverend Dr. Cecelia Williams Bryant, senior missionary supervisor of the African Methodist Episcopal Church, sponsored a mission trip in 2010 after the hurricane in Haiti. She could not get into Haiti at the time, so she planned a Youth Mission Trip to the Dominican Republic. This trip was designed to show young people how to witness to the world, particularly to those not as fortunate as we are in America. Being that my wife was missionary president and I had experience as a youth pastor, I went along as a chaperone. I was blessed to see, firsthand, the many young lives that were transformed in the ten days we were there. I saw young ladies pouring cement and wiring walls as they rebuilt a church. I saw young boys shaving the faces of residents in the senior-citizens home and talking to those seniors in another language. I saw the lives of these young people change as they ministered to the orphans at the homes we visited and sponsored. And, to tell you the truth, I don't know who was impacted the most, the people we were witnessing to or those of us doing the witnessing.

I will never forget one young lady taking her cell phone out of her bag to call her mother in the middle of our visit to the refugee plantation, where we stopped to distribute clothing and other items. I overheard her conversation with her mother:

"Momma, it's me, I just want to say that I am so sorry. I have taken my whole life for granted. I love you, Mom."

I swallowed hard as I fought back the tears. For the first time in my life, I too observed true witnessing. All the ministering I had done before could not compare or prepare me for that experience.

Dr. C is a blessing for and from God, and that experience in the Dominican Republic will be one of the most memorable experiences of my life.

But, you don't have to leave home or go to a foreign land to do good, meaningful witnessing. That can happen right where you are. Let's consider the possibility that God has even assigned a soul just for you to save. They may be outside your door just waiting and needing someone to say a kind word to them. But, if you do nothing, they may wind up in an alley, strung out on drugs or in prison for some misdeeds, all because you said nothing to them.

Now, my friend, witnessing to someone does not mean you have to preach. As we discussed earlier, witnessing could be just having someone observe you walking and working in the spirit without saying a word. Remember, you must do something to be called a disciple of Christ, a witness or ambassador by Christ.

So, get up out of your seat, somebody is waiting, somebody wants, somebody needs to be saved, and only you can do it, so...

"Be a servant with a purpose."

CLAIMING YOUR INHERITANCE

"A GATEWAY TO A RICH AND FULFILLING LIFE"

CHAPTER THREE

HEALTH

Being an Able Vessel

Therefore, I urge you, brother, in view of God's mercy, to offer your bodies as living sacrifices, holy and pleasing to God—this is your spiritual act of worship.

Romans 12:1

What if I told you that your body was a vessel owned by God but on loan to you for your earthly journey? What you do for and to God's vessel is your response to HIM giving you life. Tell me, are you blessing God through your living? Are you telling HER, by the way you take care of your body, that you are grateful for life and thankful for the chance to live for our Creator? Or are you showing discontentment and ungratefulness of the vessel that God has given you? Maybe discontentment is too strong of a word.

Don't you know that you yourselves are God's temple and that God's Spirit dwells in your midst? If anyone destroys God's temple, God will destroy that person; for God's temple is sacred, and you together are that temple.

1 Corinthians 3:16–17

So, let me put it this way. Are you expressing apathy or unconcern for your health by taking an inactive role in your physical condition?

What you put in your body speaks volumes to God as to what you think about your body, your life, and your earthly journey. I don't believe we are very conscious of how we treat the body that God has given to us. But, how we treat our bodies has a direct effect on our ministries, our witness, our service, and, eventually, our blessings.

We cannot service and please God through our living if we are in ill health. Some medical doctors believe that over 50 percent of our illnesses are preventable. Now, I'm not a medical expert who can verify those figures, but if that is half true, it means that many of our illnesses come from us not taking care of ourselves or not making good choices for our bodies.

Romans 12 tell us that part of our service, love, witness, and ministry depends on our sacrifice to God. We must be willing to take care of ourselves in order to be that living sacrifice to God, which is our reasonable service. In other words, this should be a no-brainer for us. We should want our bodies to be fully functional and ready to serve God.

The Apostle Paul wrote to the Church of Corinth:

Do you not know that your body is a temple of the Holy Spirit, who is in you, whom you have received from God? You are not your own; you were bought at a price. Therefore honor God with your body.

1 Corinthians 6:19–20

If your body is a temple of the Holy Spirit, it sounds like we are to cherish, nurture, protect, and love our body as we love any temple of God. If our body is a temple, it commands your love, affection, nurturing, and caring. When Paul used the term "temple," he was saying, in a figurative sense, that our bodies are the closest things we possess that is of God. Now, beloved, we certainly do not desire to mistreat the LORD or anything that belongs to the LORD. So, why do we mistreat our body? What we put in it affects it; how we treat it affects it. If we don't treat the temple right, it cannot function the way it was designed to function. That's what illness does; it prevents our bodies from functioning the way our bodies were designed to function.

Dear friend, I pray that you may enjoy good health and that all may go well with you, even as your soul is getting along well.

3 John, verse 2

We all want to prosper, but here the scripture is telling us that our soul's prosperity is connected to our body's prosperity. In other words, we cannot truly prosper in bad health. God wants us healthy, just as HE wants us holy. What if I told you that true prosperity, true wealth, and true success cannot be obtained with bad health? You can have all the money in the world, but with ill health, money will become meaningless. So, here is something that even the poorest among us can do that will result in our listing among the richest: *be in good health*.

I am not a physician, so what I am about to say is only a layman's hypothesis. But, for the most part, you can control over 50 percent of your health outcomes. To me, beloved, that number is high enough to peak my interest. I learned that there are seven key indicators for good health, which I will review with you in the following pages.

BLOOD PRESSURE

This indicator is major and so very easy to monitor. All it takes is a periodical reading. Some people may vary, but the average blood-pressure reading is to be less than 120/80. This can be controlled by regular exercise and proper diet. In some cases, medication is required, but it is desirable to have your pressure under control at all times. This was one of my problems. My blood pressure averaged around 140/90 when I decided to do something about it.

My doctor put me on medication, and my reading decreased to an average of 130/84. Although that was acceptable for my doctor, it was not acceptable for me. So, after reading articles and magazines and attending lectures, I started the following program, with my doctor's approval:

a.   Drinking sixty-four ounces of water per day. Boy was this hard. It was like I was drinking a river each day. But, I was determined, so I would start by drinking one, sixteen-ounce bottle of water before leaving home in the mornings. Then I gradually increased it to thirty-two ounces, which took me about a year. Do I forget to drink my thirty-two ounces of water at times? Yep, sure do, but some days I can reach my ultimate goal of sixty-four ounces, but I average around thirty-two ounces.

b. The second thing I did was to start an exercise plan. I first walked on my treadmill for sixteen minutes every other day except Sunday (my Sabbath). Again, I had to work at it. Each week, I would add a minute. Yes, I hit and missed, but eventually, after about a year, I was up to sixty minutes three times a week. Now I am not a marathon runner, and I barely walk at a respectable speed. I clock around three miles an hour, so as you can see, I am not a Jessie Owens or a Carl Lewis, but I understand the key is to move.

c. The third thing I had to do was to cut out the salt, or sodium. Now, you need to understand that I was a "salt-a-holic" (that's my made-up word). I was one of those people who puts salt on everything before I even tasted my food. Well, it was a long journey, but I eventually got it under some form of control.

I first switched from regular salt to sea salt, which means I went from 500 milligrams of sodium per quarter teaspoon to 360 milligrams of sodium per quarter teaspoon. But, my ND (Nutritional Doctor) was not satisfied and recommended Liquid Aminos, which is an all-purpose seasoning made from soy protein. It has about 160 milligrams of sodium per half teaspoon.

With those three combinations, my blood-pressure reading was reduced to an average of 128/78. This is still not good enough to write home about, but I am off the medication, and the reading is still decreasing after about a year on the program. Do I fall off the wagon at times? You bet, but my blood-pressure reading has encouraged me to stay with the plan. Now that I am off the medication, I feel I can go on.

Now, I realize that everyone is different. Please talk to your doctor. I made the decision to go to a nutritional doctor because I did not want to just treat the symptoms; I wanted to prevent the condition. I wanted my temple to be the best it can be.

SUGAR OR TRIGLYCERIDE

It is my understanding that triglyceride levels are one major indicator of developing diabetes. I understand the medical professionals like to see this number below 150. That has not been a problem for me because of my upbringing. You see, we were so poor that we could not afford many sweets or desserts, so I grew up not looking for a lot of sweets. Today, I may have one dessert per week.

But my ND had me give up a favorite of mine for preventative measures. I love Kool-Aid, which was a no-no for her, so I had to wean myself from it. Boy, I still miss that drink. She replaced it with Emergen-C, which is a dietary supplement that has twenty-four nutrients and seven B vitamins. It comes in different flavors, including Triple Berry, which has antioxidants and electrolytes, along with 1,000 milligrams of vitamin C (I still miss my Kool-Aid). By the way, I have not had a cold since.

CHOLESTEROL

Most of us know that we need to keep our cholesterol level below two hundred. But what I discovered was the need to know my LDL and my HDL cholesterol readings. I learned that your LDL is the bad cholesterol that contributes to clogged arteries. That reading should be less than 130. But you also have HDL cholesterol, which is the good cholesterol that combats the LDL. If you have HDL of forty-five or more, you are helping keep your LDL in check. Of course, it depends on how high that LDL is in the first place. I was surprised when I learned that my total cholesterol reading was 212. But, my doctor ran a more detailed blood test to find that I have a high level of HDL (about 80) to combat my LDL, which was 120, so I was all good. But, it was a shocker when I learned that our overall cholesterol reading was a combination of both HDL and LDL. So, you may want to discuss this with your doctor on your next visit.

BODY MASS INDEX (BMI)

Now, this is one area with which I do have a problem. I understand that Body Mass Index (BMI) is a reading of your body composition that indicates whether you are overweight and need to be dieting. The ideal BMI is less than twenty-five.

Would you believe I am five feet, seven inches tall and 165 pounds? For all intents and purposes, I am a puny little guy; as a matter of fact, some people call me skinny. But, with those measurements, my BMI indicator was 25.68, which meant I was slightly overweight. I didn't believe it. Me, overweight! Give me a break! But after one year on the above plan, my weight is down to 150, which lowered my BMI to twenty-three.

EXERCISE

Here, we need to just keep moving. It is recommended that we exercise for thirty minutes three times a week. Because of my war on sodium and high blood pressure, I have gone a little beyond that point. But, beloved, we all need to exercise regularly. The more we exercise the better shape we find ourselves. The most important indicator is energy. If we are too tired to do anything, how can we do the work of the LORD?

I think it is the Celebrex commercial that says, "A body in motion stays in motion." So we need to get in motion for the LORD. And God will bless us with the ability to stay in motion. This is one of those things that we can see the results of right away. If you exercise one day and rest the other but continue to exercise the third day, it becomes easier. But, if we stop and do not exercise, it becomes very difficult for us to move. Our body tells us right away when we do or do not exercise.

CALORIES

If I had to pick one area that was the most challenging for me and will likely be for you, it would be counting calories. Most Americans have a major problem controlling caloric intake, and I am no exception. When I look at the back of my food packages, I find that two thousand calories can add up very quickly. What's most frustrating for me is knowing that we can't burn two thousand calories in a day if we don't exercise. The average person may burn 1,800 calories per day without exercise, and 2,000 calories when they exercise thirty minutes three times a week. So, if a person doesn't exercise and they maintain a two thousand–calorie diet, and believe me, it will feel like a diet, that person will still gain 200 calories per day, or 73,000 calories per year. It takes 3,500 retained calories to result in a gained pound, so that person will gain approximately twenty pounds in a year.

I was reading an article by Bruce Horovitz in *USA Today* (May 17, 2012). The writer claimed that 96 percent of chain restaurant entrees exceeded the United States Department of Agriculture's (USDA) recommended limits. These USDA-recommended limits were used to evaluate main entrees from the major chains. The USDA recommends that entrees should be no more than 667 calories—35 percent of the calories from fat and 10 percent of calories from saturated fat and 767 milligrams of sodium. A whopping 96 percent of the main entrees sold at top US chain eateries exceed that daily limit. All the time, I thought fast-food restaurants were the worst, but, according to this article, "Entrees at family-style restaurants, on average, have more calories, fat, and sodium than fast-food restaurants. Entrees at family-style eateries posted 271 more calories, 435 more milligrams of sodium, and 16 more grams of fat than fast-food restaurants."

If one was to go to the restaurants tested and share an appetizer, have an average entrée, and even share a dessert, that one meal, on the average, would cost them 1,400 calories. If that same person previously had a light breakfast of just 300 calories and a conservative lunch of another 500 calories, they would have exceeded the daily recommended calorie limit by 200 calories, or 73,000 calories per year, or another twenty pounds. If you are not active, this would mean you have just gained forty pounds for the year, and you will be loaded with sodium and saturated fat. What is the best solution? Eat at home! And exercise!

TESTS AND SCREENING

Most of us do not have perfect bodies. We need to stay on top of our health and monitor what is going on into our bodies. To do this, we need to visit our doctors regularly. I personally believe in preventive medicine, so I have two doctors: a regular MD and an ND If my MD doesn't work with my ND or my ND rejects what my MD is saying, I will change doctors. I tell my doctors up front that I have a personal interest in my body. I keep track of my screening and tests, and I discuss the outcomes. I ask questions and expect answers. After all, this is my body that God has given to me. I believe the better I treat this body, the better it will perform for me. My doctors understand that, and I will not waste their time by failing to follow their instructions. If I have a problem with their instructions, I will tell them then, and we will come to an understanding.

The only way you are going to know your body is to test it and review the results with your physician. I know you would rather not because you don't want to hear bad news about your health. Well, if it is bad news, you not knowing will not make it better. Testing may give you one up on the illness that you want to prevent and at least change or minimize its effect. I am not writing this to frighten you but to encourage you to take charge of your life. Take an interest in your health. It is the only way you can thank God for life, and do whatever you can to make this life the best you can.

If you have a family history of certain conditions, now is the time to look into it. The medical field has made so many advancements in treatment and even finding cures.

Why not get a jump on your family history and eliminate what was a curse. Only your active participation can make the difference; your inactive attitude can only make things worse.

But, I do want to encourage you to go a step further by seeking the services of a nutritional doctor. I believe with all my heart that there are preventative medical measures that you and I can take to eliminate what our ancestors have gone through. You are blessed to be here at a time when research has given us so much more information and resources, which we cannot afford to ignore.

SEVENTH-DAY ADVENTIST

Although I am not a Seventh-Day Adventist, I admire their approach to stewardship of the body.

In a 2009 article in *U.S. News & World Report*, Deborah Kotz noted:

"Members of the denomination have an average life expectancy of eighty-nine, about a decade longer than the average American. One of the basic tenants of the religion is that it's important to cherish the body that's on loan from God, which means no smoking, alcohol, or overindulging in sweets. Followers typically stick to a vegetarian diet based on fruits, vegetables, beans, and nuts, with plenty of exercise. They're also very focused on family and community."

I have a friend who is a Seventh-Day Adventist, and if knowing her made any difference, let me tell you, I am sold on their diet. She is between five to ten years my senior but reminds me of Lena Horne or Sophia Loren. Her skin is firm and smooth, and you have to admire her excellent physical shape, not in a sexual way but because you know she has taken care of herself and gives glory to God. Her husband is equally impressive (as I turn green). He is a handsome, stately gentleman with energy and zest that let you know the two of them are definitely doing something right.

I visited a Seventh-Day Adventist church and was amazed at what I saw. Now, there were people there who appeared to be overweight, but, for the most part, there seemed to be a large number of people who were slim, very healthy, and nice looking. I remember being invited to dinner after the Worship Service. I was surprised at the food that appeared to be meat, but it was actually soy products that tasted tremendous. I remember asking for the recipe because the food was so delicious.

Now, I did not convert my diet right away. Do you know why? I was listening to the hype about our bodies needing protein and the only good source of protein being from animal meat. But, the more I saw people being diagnosed with diseases like cancer, heart conditions, and diabetes that have very low occurrences among people with plant-based diets, I began to wonder. Maybe, just maybe there was something to this diet. Then I had a conversation with my niece, who is a pediatrician. She agreed that there is something to a plant-based diet. She started to share information with me and encouraged me to read more and research before I started changing my diet. She had me watch a film entitled *Food, Inc.*, and that did it for me (by the way, don't watch the film on a full stomach).

Dr. T. Colin Campbell, along with his colleague and son Thomas M Campbell II, MD, published a book entitled *The China Study* that documented research materials collected over forty years. Although the presentation is lengthy about why one should consider a plant-based diet, these are some of his key arguments for why one should make the switch. Dr. Campbell states...

"The American people need to know the truth. They need to know what we have uncovered in our research. People need to know why we are unnecessarily sick, why too many of us die early despite the billions spent on research. The irony is that the solution is simple and inexpensive. The answer to the American health crisis is the food that each of us chooses to put in our mouths each day. It's as simple as that."

He further states, "If you are only interested in a two-week menu plan to lose weight, then this book is not for you. I am appealing to your intelligence, not to your ability to follow a recipe or menu plan. I want to offer you a more profound and more beneficial way to view health. I have a prescription for maximum health that is simple, easy to follow, and offers more benefit than any drug or surgery, without any of the side effects. This prescription isn't merely a menu plan; it doesn't require daily charts or calorie counting; and it doesn't exist to serve my own financial interests. Most importantly, the supporting evidence is overwhelming. This is about changing the way you eat and live and the extraordinary health that will result.

"So, what is my prescription for good health? In short, it is about the multiple health benefits of consuming plant-based foods and the largely unappreciated health dangers of consuming animal-based foods, including all types of meat, dairy, and eggs. I did not begin with preconceived ideas, philosophical or otherwise, to prove the worthiness of plant-based diets. I started at the opposite end of the spectrum: as a meat-loving dairy farmer in my personal life and an 'establishment' scientist in my professional life. I even used to lament the views of vegetarians as I taught nutritional biochemistry to premed students."

Beloved, here is a man who spent his entire life studying diseases, illnesses, and the deaths of people in America and Asia.

This man grew up on a dairy farm and initially favored the beef and dairy products that his family produced and sold, which provided their livelihood. But, after years of researching and studying people, cultures, and diets, he made a complete change. Why? Is he full of it or just plain off his rocker? No, I don't think so. Rather, he learned something about living. I believe there is something to be said about the plant-based diet, and I invite you to look further. Read, research, ask questions; after all, it is your body, your health, and your life.

On December 3, 2012, reporter Amelia Clabots posted an interview with Dr. Dan Buettner, a *National Geographic* scientist who spent years studying the living habits of a person of the "Blue Zone." These are areas of the world where it is not unusual for a person to live beyond one hundred years of age. Dr. Buettner shared five key lifestyle traits that were unveiled.

1. Being Social:
   Being around positive people and those you love and admire has a positive effect on your health. Laughter and enjoying others is somewhat like medicine.
2. Staying active:

Although most of the people in the study did not go to the gym or have a thirty- to sixty-minute workout, being active by just moving was essential to their health.

3. Daily Downtime:
   Pray, meditation, or just napping seem to add to good health.
4. Live with Purpose:
   Have a zeal for life. A person living with purpose has reason to rise and move.
5. Diet:
   You are right! Plant-based diet.

The American Institute for Cancer Research has another list of recommendations for cancer prevention. Although their intent is to reduce your risk in developing cancer, I believe these step are effective in our overall health as well:

1. *Be as lean as possible without becoming underweight.*
   I believe this can be done by maintaining a Body Mass Index of twenty-five or less.
2. *Be physically active for at least thirty minutes every day.*
   You can also obtain a pedometer and set a goal of 10,000 steps per day. But most importantly, do your best to keep moving.
3. *Avoid sugary drinks. Limit consumption of energy-dense foods (particularly processed foods high in added sugar, low in fiber, or high in fat).*
   I stopped ordering any drinks at the restaurant except water with no ice. I don't buy soda anymore because of the sugar content.
4. *Eat more of a variety of vegetables, fruits, whole grains, and legumes such as beans.*
   I still use my parents' Louisiana recipe of red beans and rice, but I use brown rice instead. I have given myself a goal to have fruit for my desert.

5. *Limit consumption of red meats (such as beef, pork, and lamb), and avoid processed meats.*

    As you can decipher, I am leaning toward a plant-based diet. All of the medical research I have read and hearing people recite their doctors' recommendation have pointed toward reducing or eliminating meat.

    If consumed at all, limit alcoholic drinks to two for men and one for women a day.

    I don't drink at all, and maybe this information can convince you as well.

6. *Limit consumption of salty foods and foods processed with salt (sodium).*

    I stopped buying canned foods, which are loaded with sodium. Invest in sea salt and other spices and herbs to reduce your sodium intake.

7. *Don't use supplements to protect against cancer.*

    Now, this I did not know. You may want to do more research on this, but with the other health-style adoptions, you may not have this concern unless cancer is part of your family history.

8. *Eliminate your use of tobacco.*

    If you don't smoke, please don't start. I experienced some respiratory complication in the past, and the only thing the doctors could agree on was that I was a victim of secondhand smoke. My father was a smoker and a drinker, and they hypothesized that it affected my breathing. So, at least for your children and those who live around you, please don't smoke.

Remember, beloved:

Do you not know that your body is a temple of the Holy Spirit, who is in you, whom you have received from God? You are not your own; you were bought at a price. Therefore honor God with your body.

1 Corinthians 6:19–20

TREAT YOUR BODY AS GOD'S TEMPLE
"IT'S ALL YOU HAVE"

Reactive Article

As a physician, I am acutely aware of the consequences of our lifestyle choices. These outcomes are reflected most obviously in our personal temples but also reveal themselves in our families, neighborhoods, church body, and society. I completely agree that to be an excellent living sacrifice to God, we must care for our bodies and ward off disease.

Most diseases of the Western world are preventable. Our bodies in their healthiest state are made to maintain that healthy state. Though the specifics of this chapter are helpful, the simplest way to keep our temples in optimal shape is proper diet and exercise. The diet I recommend is best stated by author Michael Pollan, "Eat food, not too much, mostly plants." For exercise, I recommend thirty to sixty minutes of aerobic activity most days of the week. Just a few simple changes in awareness and daily practice can make each of us an able vessel of God.

La Donna J. Johnson, MD
Website: PamperedLivingAFC.com
E-mail: PamperedLivingAFC@gmail.com
Telephone: 248-783-6AFC

Reactive Article

The six principles upon which naturopathic medicine is founded are: let nature heal, treat the whole person, do no harm, treat the cause, educate the patient, and prevent illnesses.

High Blood Pressure

There may be many different reasons why someone has high blood pressure. Since everyone is different, figuring out the underlying cause will lead to a more effective treatment and positive outcome.

Triglycerides

Triglycerides are a type of fat that can originate from food, particularly simple carbohydrates also known as simple sugars. The body uses simple sugar as a source of energy and stores excess sugar as triglycerides. If triglycerides become too high and not able to be broken down in the blood stream, it builds up, gets stored, causes inflammation, and may lead to an increased risk of diseases, diabetes, and heart attacks, to name a few.

I believe that a well-balanced immune system starts with a healthy gut. A large number of the body's defense comes from our gastrointestinal tract (our gut). Excessive amounts of simple sugar (simple carbohydrate) may contribute to chronic inflammation within our body. Remember, our body converts simple sugar into energy, but whatever is left over may turn into triglycerides and lead to increased inflammation. Cutting back on sugar can be simple: read labels and look for ingredients like corn syrup, high-fructose corn syrup, sucrose, glucose, fructose, maltose, table sugar, fruit juices, honey, molasses, and brown sugar.

Cholesterol

Certain amounts of cholesterol are needed for our bodies to work properly. Excessive amounts can cause clogged arteries. Different types of cholesterol play different roles. *Bad* LDL carries cholesterol and some fats to different areas of the body. Excess amounts of LDL in the blood stream will increase your chances of having heart diseases. *Good* HDL carries cholesterol from the blood stream to the liver to be degraded, preventing clogged arteries.

Total cholesterol is the combination of HDL, LDL, and triglycerides. It can be used to assess the risk of heart disease but should not be the only indicator. It is important to measure LDL, HDL, and triglyceride levels. I often recommend those who have elevated cholesterol to eat a plant-based diet, as studies have shown vegans have lower cholesterol levels compared to carnivores. Eating a plant-based diet especially high in soluble fiber may have a dramatic cholesterol-lowering effect

Exercise

Being in motion increases respiration and circulation. Thus, more oxygen and nutrients are delivered to the tissue, and waste products are removed more quickly when exercising. Exercising on a regular basis may relieve stress and enhance overall well-being.

Lifestyle

Little decisions, like the foods we choose to eat at meals and the activities we choose to participate in, may affect our health the most. I like to take the time to review the lifestyle of every person and make recommendations to substitute healthier habits for old habits that may be disease forming.

I recommend eating fresh, organic, and locally grown foods. Food in its whole form contains essential vitamins and nutrients that may be lost in processing methods.

I believe the key to maintaining optimal health is to understand our bodies. However, most medical issues that are discovered on blood tests cannot be felt. The only way to learn of these potential problems is by doing blood work and getting routine physical exams.

Being proactive may improve quality of life and prevent future illnesses.

Nhung V. Nguyen, ND LAc
Natural Health, LLC

Naturopathic Medicine, Acupuncture & Oriental Medicine
6500—67th Street
Kenosha, WI 53142
Telephone: 262-764-2012
E-mail: info@drvnguyen.com
Website: www.drvnguyen.com

Reactive Article

From a Seventh-Day Adventist point of view:

It is said that in the Garden of Eden, Adam and Eve thrived beautifully on a wide source of fruits and vegetables. Many years later, God destroyed the entire earth with a flood, and when man was able to walk the earth again, there was no vegetation to supply his source of food. Perhaps this was the introduction of meat into the main stream of our menu. Romans 14:17 says, "For the kingdom of God is not meat and drink, but righteousness and peace, and joy in the Holy Spirit."

As a practicing Seventh-Day Adventist, I agree with the earlier quotes from Deborah Kotz, who shared that a major part of our diet should be based on fruits, vegetables, beans, and nuts. I remember from early childhood that beans, nuts, and peanut butter were an important source of protein that is vital to our growth and health. Plants grown for food are an important part of God's creation. It is true that statistics show that the lifestyle of the Seventh-Day Adventists may result in a longer life.

In the August 9, 2012, issue of *Adventist Review* is an interesting article entitled, "Closer to the Source," in which an eighty-two-year-old organic farmer, Arnold Schmidt, speaks about the merits of growing one's own seed, rotating crops, and not using insecticides on the wheat being used for bread. He also referenced the days gone by when the majority of what Americans ate was raised from their own gardens, pastures, and fields. Despite the fact that those days are primarily in the past, we are responsible for providing our families with well balanced meals.

Most Adventists are vegetarians who plan and serve delicious menus. One source of delightful recipes comes from a recipe book entitled, *Seasoned with Love, A Second Helping* (edited by Sharon M. Cress). This is a collection of pastoral wives' favorite recipes.

Those of us who include meat and fish in our menu acknowledge the fact that, according to our teaching, we do not eat seafood from the bottom of the sea (such as shrimp, oysters, lobsters, and fish without scales—e.g., catfish—but we do enjoy flounder, tilapia, bass, and such). In addition, we enjoy fowl, such as chicken and turkey, to name a few. I believe a well-balanced meal with vegetables, meat, fruit, and a minimal amount of dessert would add years to any person's life, especially a Seventh-Day Adventist.

Juanita P. Kemp, PhD
Southern Asian Seventh-Day Adventist Church
Silver Spring, MD 20904
E-mail: juankemp@verizon.com

CHAPTER FOUR

ECONOMICS

Christian Economics in a Capitalistic Society

There is one area of our lives that can give witness to our blessings. It is often expressed in monetary terms but is dependent on our stewardship. Yes, I am speaking to the area of our lives we often pay the most attention to as a measure of our success, blessing, or prosperity. Economics is probably the most looked at measure of success, not only our individual lives but the entire country and the world. Economics is what drives the American capitalistic system, if not the entire world, and it is the basis for practically every war, negotiation for peace, and treaty ever signed. Even in our personal lives, how we stand economically can determine how we rank in our families, neighborhoods, clubs, associations, and, yes, even churches, the latter of which is most unfortunate.

What makes this dangerous is that I believe we put too much emphasis on economics (which is mostly measured by money) and not enough on what really makes life meaningful. I agree that in this country, money talks, and without it, life can be quite challenging if not downright difficult. But money gives us false beliefs and the illusion that it can fix it all. I was watching CNN where Piers Morgan was interviewing the Dalai Lama. As you know, he is considered the Highest Priest of Tibetan Buddhism.

Wikipedia says:

"In religious terms, the Dalai Lama is believed, by his devotees, to be the rebirth of a long line of tulkus who are considered to be manifestations of the bodhisattva of compassion. The Dalai Lama is thought of as the latest reincarnation of a series of spiritual leaders who have *chosen* to be reborn in order to enlighten others."

Now, before you get upset, thinking that I am embracing beliefs outside of Christianity, please stay with me. I believe I can articulate the enlightened thoughts of those who embrace this concept to bring to you to a better understanding of Christianity. I believe Christ is the incarnated *word* that was made flesh in Jesus of Nazareth. I believe he represented not only a rebirth of prophets but also a complete mani-festation of the *word wisdom* and the persona of God *The* Creator. So, walk with me here.

On April 25, 2012, the Dalai Lama mentioned (and I am paraphras-ing) that to focus on material things can actually subtract from the Spirit. Why? Because the Spirit is exclusive and cannot share in the attention of flesh or matter. He further stated that true peace, true happiness, and true contentment come from within. Wow! That sounds like John 14:23–27:

Jesus replied, "If anyone loves me, he will obey my teaching. My Father will love him, and we will come to him and make our home with him. He who does not love me will not obey my teaching. These words you hear are not my own; they belong to the Father who sent me. All this I have spoken while still with you. But the Counselor, the Holy Spirit, whom the Father will send in my name, will teach you all things and will remind you of everything I have said to you. Peace I leave with you; my peace I give you. I do not give to you as the world gives. Do not let your hearts be troubled and do not be afraid."

If life could be measured by money alone, man (particularly those who have lots of money) would be able to fix all things. Money would be able to give you all you need for a successful and fulfilled life. If that were the case, no millionaire would ever commit suicide. But, as you know, that is not true. You probably know a number of people who have plenty of money and are financially set, yet appear to be unhappy.

You may have asked yourself, "So-and-so has so much going for himself or herself, I wonder why they seem so unhappy?"

Well, my friend, money is not everything. Money is a tool, just like the talent(s) that the servants received in Matthew's 25:14–30 passages, but money cannot afford you true success or true happiness. Let's review what Christ taught in Matthew 6:25–34:

Therefore I tell you, do not worry about your life, what you will eat or drink; or about your body, what you will wear. Is not life more important than food, and the body more important than clothes? Look at the birds of the air; they do not sow or reap or store away in barns, and yet your heavenly Father feeds them. Are you not much more valuable than they? Who of you by worrying can add a single hour to [your] life?

And why do you worry about clothes? See how the lilies of the field grow. They do not labor or spin. Yet I tell you that not even Solomon in all his splendor was dressed like one of these. If that is how God clothes the grass of the field, which is here today and tomorrow is thrown into the fire, will he not much more clothe you, O you of little faith? So do not worry, saying, 'What shall we eat?' or 'What shall we drink?' or 'What shall we wear?' For the pagans run after all these things, and your heavenly Father knows that you need them. But seek first His kingdom and His righteousness, and all these things will be given to you as well. Therefore do not worry about tomorrow, for tomorrow will worry about itself. Each day has enough trouble of its own.

I believe those with money can be unhappy because they are struggling with something that money cannot resolve. Many psychological, social, or biological issues with which we struggle are not solvable by throwing money at them. In some cases, money can worsen the situation. As we discussed before, money is a tool. If you use the wrong tool, you can sometimes make matters worse or even create new problems for yourself or others. I believe some people have problems because they do not put first things first. They place too much emphasis on the wrong thing.

Christ is not saying that we should not be concerned about what to eat, drink, or wear but, rather, these should not be our central focus where you enter into a state of worry. Worry takes over our thinking and can blind us from matters that are before us. When we worry, we actually become unproductive and achieve very little. Worrying can also cause anxieties and even ailments that increase our delay in managing matters. This often makes matters worse. Christ is telling us that worry is totally undesirable for the Christian and really has no place in our vocabulary. But if you focus on the one who made and sent us, he will also provide for us; so don't worry about it, just focus on doing God's will in your lives. Once you do that, God will take care of the rest, and even more. Remember, God made you for HER glory; HE wants you to be successful. God wants to show you off to the world because you are Jehovah's. However, we must put our faith in HER and not think like the world or worry about tomorrow, especially worldly things that are worries of pagans.

Remember, worry is totally unproductive. You can change nothing by worrying. You can't solve a single problem by worrying. As a matter of fact, worrying is counterproductive and takes away your peace of mind. You become a victim of circumstances rather than victorious over situations or matters.

As the scripture reminds us, we cannot change one hair on our head by worrying, but we can cause hair to fall out, which is counterproductive. So, my friend, try to eliminate the word "worry" from your vocabulary, and start focusing on what really matters: the will of God.

But remember the LORD, your God, for it is He who gives you the ability to produce wealth, and so confirms his covenant, which he swore to your forefathers, as it is today.

Deuteronomy 8:18

Today there are major misconceptions about finances circulating in the church, leading Christians to believe that God will take care of all of our financial problems with the wave of HIS hand, without regard to the guidelines He has already given in HIS WORD. These misconceptions about God's economic system are preventing many Christians form receiving Jehovah's supernatural blessings in their lives.

First of all, we need to dispel some myths about money and wealth in our Christian walk.

As Jesus started on his way, a man ran up to him and fell on his knees before him. "Good teacher," he asked, "what must I do to inherit eternal life?" "Why do you call me good?" Jesus answered. "No one is good–except God alone. You know the commandments: 'Do not murder, do not commit adultery, do not steal, do not give false testimony, do not defraud, honor your father and mother.'" "Teacher," he declared, "all these I have kept since I was a boy."

Jesus looked at him and loved him. "One thing you lack," he said. "Go, sell everything you have and give to the poor, and you will have treasure in heaven. Then come, follow me." At this the man's face fell. He went away sad, because he had great wealth. Jesus looked around and said to his disciples, "How hard it is for the rich to enter the kingdom of God!" The disciples were amazed at his words. But Jesus said again, "Children, how hard it is to enter the kingdom of God! It is easier for a camel to go through the eye of a needle than for a rich man to enter the kingdom of God." The disciples were even more amazed, and said to each other, "Who then can be saved?" Jesus looked at them and said, "With man this is impossible, but not with God; all things are possible with God."

Mark 10:17–27

All through my childhood, I heard the scriptures being used to partially condemn the rich and pacify the poor. Poverty was legitimized or validated as being a gateway to holiness. It appeared to me that all preachers and teachers were telling us that it was all right to be poor and that it was somewhat righteous and holy. Beloved, fortunately, that is not what Christ was saying at all.

Christ's experience was with a very rich person who he perceived was very *attached* to his riches and could not fully service God because of this *attachment* to his wealth. When he gave the scenario of a camel entering into an eye of a needle, he was making reference to the needle or entrance to a tent. In order for a camel to enter the tent, the camel had to kneel, or humble itself.

Humbling oneself was difficult then, and in many cases still is very hard for a rich person, because many are so dependent on their riches. I am not saying it is impossible, but it may be very difficult for them to do.

But, if that very same man had trusted in the LORD, he could have sold his riches and may have become one of the disciples because Jesus did ask him to come back and follow him.

The second misunderstanding is that Jesus had a great deal of animosity for rich people. This is not true. Some of the twelve disciples being trained to be apostles were people of means, like the Zebedee brothers, Peter and Matthew, and maybe more. We just don't know enough about them. He challenged the rich man because he saw the attachment he had to his riches. The lesson is designed to let us know that we cannot serve God and be attached to materialistic things like money, items, and status because they may become the central focus in our lives. Does this mean Christ wants us poor? *Absolutely not!* But he does not want us to be enslaved by finances either.
The scripture also says:

I have raised my hand to the LORD, God Most High, Creator of heaven and earth, and have taken an oath that I will accept nothing belonging to you, not even a thread or the thong of a sandal, so that you will never be able to say, "I made Abram rich."

Genesis 14:22–23

Abram was saying this to a king. Here we see that Abram did get rich, but his riches came from the LORD. This is very significant because it tells us that God can bring us all to wealth, but in such a way that man will know it was God and not man. This passage of scripture also confirms that wealth is not a problem for God; HE does not care how much you have accumulated. As a matter of fact, SHE is willing to bless you with more. But, we must first seek God's will in our lives. Everything we do should be leaning toward the glory of God.

If we seek first the kingdom of God, all other blessings will be ours, including wealth. Beloved, God does not want us poor. God wants us to be rich, but in more ways than money, status, and earthly resources. If we put Jehovah first, HE will give us what money cannot buy: love, peace, joy, comfort, and more.

There's a third misunderstanding that we have been taught about having money. It arises from the misinterpretation and twisting of scripture. Remember the saying, "Money is the root of all evil?" Well, here is what the Bible actually says:

For the love of money is a root of all kinds of evil.

1 Timothy 6:10a

Maybe I did not listen well, but it sure seemed to me that I was being taught that money causes all sorts of evil. But, it is the *love* of money that makes humans go crazy. Humans will steal, kill, lie, deceive, go to war, destroy careers and lives of innocent people, put poison in food, put dangerous material in construction, and all sorts of evil things just for a bigger profit.

Can you imagine betraying someone that you are supposed to love for thirty pieces of silver? Some have sold their bodies, some have sold their belongings, and some have even sold their own children, all for the pagan's almighty dollar.

Our government is just as bad, if not worse. Governments have instituted the lotteries and approved gambling casinos just to raise revenues, even though it has been proven that these activities lead to individuals destroying their own lives. People spend millions each week just for the chance (with extremely poor odds) to win a pot of money that they realistically won't win in a thousand attempts. The practice becomes habit forming to the point of financial, and even life, destruction.

We have lobbyists who wine and dine our lawmakers and provide nothing but legalized bribes. These lawmakers really think the public does not know that they are buying votes and favors. For the almighty dollar, we will send common or poor people's sons and daughters to war when we know we are just claiming oil and other rights to make more money and leave communities stripped of their land and resources. For the love of money, we have pretended to ignore evildoers and evil deeds and policies. What fascinate me are reality shows that are on TV now. People will go on television and disgrace their entire family for a little fame and money.

A parishioner made a statement that "investing in Wall Street was the same as playing the lottery." Beloved, I pray that, by the end of this book, you will think differently if you thought that way at all. I explained to the person that a game of chance, like the lottery, has three players: a winner, a loser, and the house. In all games of chance, the house gets a payout each and every time, so the house never loses. They may or may not have a winner, but, the others will always pay for it all; they are the losers. Investments (or playing the stock market) are not designed that way. Here, one has an investor and the company. If the company makes money, the investor does as well. The system is not designed to create losers, like the lottery or casinos. Just think, we have been brainwashed to believe we can succeed playing the lottery or gambling at a casino but not by investing in the stock market. This is terrible logic.

Let's look at economics. Many of us were taught that economics is strictly money, commerce, and the result of Wall Street. But, economics is bigger than that. It is the way we live and exchange for the things we need.

Ron Paul, in his quest for the presidency of the United States, argued (again, I paraphrase) that our economy is being ruined and that we should go back to the currency of the Confederacy, or at least a gold-controlled system, and stop printing paper currency. He believes artificial inflation is driving our economy over a financial cliff. Have you ever thought what would happen if we went back to the day of the Gold Rush and just used gold as a means of exchange? Until it becomes a universal acceptance, it will be devastating. It doesn't matter if you use gold, silver, treasury notes, or bubble gum, it has to be given a value and universally accepted as a common means of exchange. It really does not have to be backed by anything but the value that people put on that method of exchange.

But, being a good steward, you can adjust to whatever the economy uses or promotes, because you are using God's method of survival:

Go to the ant, you sluggard; consider its ways and be wise! It has no commander, no overseer or ruler, yet it stores its provisions in summer and gathers its food at harvest. How long will you lie there, you sluggard?

When will you get up from your sleep? A little sleep, a little slumber, a little folding of the hands to rest—and poverty will come on you like a bandit and scarcity like an armed man.

Proverbs 6:6–11

I was born into poverty. We were so poor that we pronounced our economic status as "PO," for we could not afford to even complete the word. Yes, welfare was our refuge but not our crutch. I mentioned that our father died when I was only nine years old and left my mother without resources, so welfare was the only way.

But she taught us to never give up or depend on welfare. She was faced with rearing six children, with the oldest being eighteen and the youngest five years old. She had a tenth-grade education at the time, but she never gave up and preached to her children to never give up either. From public housing, where helplessness was alive and well, she convinced four of her six children to go and complete college through the GI Bill, loans, part-time jobs, or a combination of the three. The most inspiring event for me occurred the year I graduated from community college with an associate's degree. My mother was also graduating from high school, having earned her GED.

What a wonderful illustration that was for me. But, that's not all; she continued her education, learning a skill that earned her a job she had until age sixty-seven. The only reason my mother retired then was because of the demands of caring for my grandparents. So, as you can see, we not only heard it from our mother, we saw it as well. Many times she told us to keep trying: "You can make it if you try." I was sort of timid, and at times wanted to give up, but this drill sergeant (which I fondly still call her today) stayed on my case, quoting scriptures like Proverbs 6:6–11 or:

I know what it is to be in need, and I know what it is to have plenty. I have learned the secret of being content in any and every situation, whether well fed or hungry, whether living in plenty or in want. I can do everything through him who gives me strength.

Philippians 4:12–13

Stewardship allows us to adjust to what the economy is dictating. Stewardship is the Christian mechanism for survival, but as we learned in Matthew 6:33, if you seek the Kingdom of God first, all these things will be given to you as well. In other words, we must live our lives to pleasure God, and he will take care of us. Does that mean he will make us rich? Maybe not in finances, but, my friend, you can be rich in so many other ways. Rest assured, God has financial riches to give as well. We need to adopt the attitude of Abraham:

Then Melchizedek, king of Salem, brought out bread and wine. He was priest of God Most High, and he blessed Abram, saying, "Blessed be Abram by God Most High, Creator of heaven and earth. And blessed by God Most High, who delivered your enemies into your hand." Then Abram gave him a tenth of everything.

Genesis 14:18–20

62

I used to have a problem with Mom giving to the church. Here we were, poorer than a church mouse, and she would bake a cake, which we very seldom had, or prepare a big pot roast, which also was a rarity in our house, and take it to the church. Here we were, with less than two sticks to rub together, and she was saving her pennies to give to the church. Do you remember the "Widow's Mite?"

As he looked up, Jesus saw the rich putting their gifts into the temple treasury. He also saw a poor widow put in two very small copper coins. "I tell you the truth," he said, "this poor widow has put in more than all the others. All these people gave their gifts out of their wealth; but she out of her poverty put in all she had to live on."

Luke 21:1–4

Now, I'm sure that my mother did not give all that we had to live on. Nor am I sure she gave a tenth of what we had, but sometimes it felt like 50 percent. She explained to us that "all things belong to the LORD," and we only give a fraction of his blessings. But, if we faithfully give unto the LORD, God will give more to us. Mother would often sing a song, written by Doris M. Akers and recorded by the Caravans in 1958, which supported her advice:

> *You can't beat God's giving*
> *No matter how you try*
> *Just as sure, as you are living*
> *And the LORD is in heaven, on high*
> *The more you give, the more HE gives to you*
> *So keep on giving, because it's really true*
> *That you can't beat God's giving*
> *No matter how you try.*

My older brother took it to another level. I learned more about stewardship from that guy than I learned in all the classes, seminars, and seminary classes I attended. My brother was not a churchgoer (even to this day), but he showed how everything belonged to the LORD (who entrusted HIS gifts to us), how one should treat the gifts, and how to determine *your* gifts and blessings. Still today, God has blessed me with resources so that I can buy as much food as I need, afford very comfortable housing (especially in a parsonage), drive a pretty nice car (a Chevrolet is just fine with me), and more than meet my needs.

I am teased for using my tea bag twice, saving my aluminum foil, and washing my plastic forks. No, I don't have to do that now, but it reminds me from where I came and how I am grateful for every little thing I've got and will never take it for granted. My brother didn't call it stewardship, he just said God gives us "survival techniques," but he also said something that made you feel that it came from the WORD OF GOD.

I even remember how my brother would *create a tithe*. You may say, "How do you create a tithe?"

Well, I'm glad you asked. He would pick up pennies and recycle materials long before it was considered being eco-friendly. Sometimes he would walk from school to save money on bus fare, just to make sure that he had money to give to Mom for church, because Mom's tithes represented her "Total Earthly Substance."

We all learned from Mom. My brothers and I would collect newspapers, roll them up, and sell them to the fish market.

We learned from that country girl that all that you receive should be a part of your tithing: your wages, investments, welfare check, anything, even that penny you found was part of your earthly substance. As I look back, I realize my mother was crazy; yes, crazy as a fox. As I look at her now at ninety-plus years old, she is in good health, wants for nothing, all of her children are independent, and none of us went to prison or faced any life-threatening illnesses. I now understand and see her as a very rich and blessed woman of God.

Will a man rob God? Yet you rob me. But you ask, "How do we rob you?"

"In tithes and offerings. You are under a curse—the whole nation of you—because you are robbing me. Bring the whole tithe into the

storehouse, that there may be food in my house. Test me in this, says the LORD ALMIGHTY, and see if I will not throw open the floodgates of heaven and pour out so much blessing that you will not have room enough for it."

Malachi 3:8–10

I believe we, as a people, are robbing God. We have become a very spoiled generation. I remember President Jimmy Carter coming under heavy criticism when he called Americans spoiled. Well, my friend, he was right. We complain because we do not have the moon.

We spend our money like there is no tomorrow and without assuming any responsibility. Yet, when it comes to giving to the one who has given us so much, we tip. Some of us are still giving one dollar in church, like it represents something other than just plain theological robbery, yet we sometimes wonder why we are not getting the things out of life that we want. It is we, not God, who block our blessings. When we withhold from God, HE has no way of returning tenfold, a hundredfold, or three hundred–fold because we gave nothing.

Each man [or woman] should give what he [or she] has decided in their heart to give, not reluctantly or under compulsion, for God loves a cheerful giver.

2 Corinthians 9:7

I love giving, especially to the LORD. But I have to make a confession; I do not consider myself a tither. Why? Because a tither is traditionally a person who gives 10 percent of his or her earthly substance. Well, I enjoy a lot of blessings, so I selfishly give more because I have learned that the more you give, the more you will receive, and I am a living witness. So, I have no problem giving.

Give, and it will be given to you. A good measure, pressed down, shaken together and running over, will be poured into your lap. For with the measure you use, it will be measured to you.

Luke 6:38

This doesn't just work with my tithes and offerings at church; this giving formula works elsewhere as well. When I see a need, and the Holy Spirit moves me to give, I don't hesitate, and just about 100 percent of the time, I don't suffer or experience hardship because of my giving. And I can almost see the blessings coming back immediately. I will give someone money, and before that week is out, I will receive unexpected funds from somewhere.

But, what makes giving so special is that sometimes I can see my prayers being answered as well. Oh, I tell you, my friend, nothing beats serving the LORD and being obedient to God's will.

Never stop tithing to the LORD. When you stop, you are saying to the LORD, "I am no longer grateful to you, nor do I trust that you will provide for me, therefore, I will take your place by providing for myself." Brothers and sisters, can you provide for yourself? Can you do it better than the LORD?

Honor the LORD with your wealth, with the first fruits of all your crops; then your barns will be filled to overflowing, and your vats will brim over with new wine.

Proverbs 3: 9–10

In his book, *God's Plans for your Finances*, Dwight Nichols writes:

"Unfortunately, many Christians believe that their stewardship responsibilities end after they have given their tithes and offerings on Sunday morning. During the remainder of the week, they deal with their finances pretty much as the rest of the world does, using the same financial concepts and principles. The Bible describes this as the world system."

He explains stewardship is also a concept of God to use each and every thing from Him as a trust from Him. How we spend our time, talent, energy, and finances reflects how we worship and serve Him.

Do not conform any longer to the pattern of this world, but be transformed by the renewing of your mind. Then you will be able to test and approve what God's will is—his good, pleasing, and perfect will.

Romans 12:2

In order to be good stewards, we must change our way of thinking about the world. We must understand we cannot live our lives like the world, make decisions like the world, and expect to have a life different than the world.

But you are a chosen people, a royal priesthood, a holy nation, a people belonging to God that you may declare the praises of him who called you out of darkness into his wonderful light.

1 Peter 2:9

You are different than the world's citizens. You have to choose to be either the Light of the World or the Life of the Party. Remember, you were born again to exhibit a different lifestyle that is meant to be *in* you. People are to see hope, joy, love, peace, and happiness, all of which do not have a worldly origin. If you chase after worldly things, your vision will become clouded with worldly things; your thoughts will become clouded with worldly thoughts; and your choices will become infected with worldly choices. Your output, performance, works, and deeds will all be worldly and of no value for the Kingdom. Beloved, you can never please God with a worldly appetite, and, guess what; you can never please yourself with a worldly appetite. Why? Because the world walks in the flesh. Remember Galatians 5: walking in the flesh produces behaviors and end results that destine a Child of God to failure. One of these activities is greed. With greed, you will never have enough. It is only with a spirit gift of self-control that you will be able to settle down to realize a blessed life.

Words of caution:

"YOU CANNOT MEASURE HEAVENLY BLESSINGS
WITH A WORLDLY YARDSTICK."

Blessings are not all material; as a matter of fact, most of your blessings are not material at all. In other words, if you try to measure God's blessing on your tithes and offerings—or any form of stewardship—with materialism or financial gains, you may miss your blessings, because not all blessings can be measured in physical terms.

I told you about my 90-plus-year-old mother and how she prayed for her children, who are all healthy, independent, and not in prison. Now you may say, that has happened to people who don't exercise stewardship, and you may be right, but as you look at one area with your eyes, you may miss two with your spirit. I believe God blessed my mother by answering her prayers, and you just can't put a price tag on that. Plus, all material things are not as much of a blessing as it seems. Some material things can cause a lot of headaches. Many material things can depreciate in value or become worthless, while other material things can just waste away.

Blessings cannot always be counted like widgets. As a matter of fact, most of our blessings are not even tangible. I gave an example of my mother's prayers being answered, and I am quite sure you can think of many examples of your own or those you know who have had something good happen in life. Sometimes it can be as small and hardly noticeable as a fleeting thought that tells you to turn early or choose another route while driving, only to find out there was an accident just at the time you would have been at that location. What about finding a job when others were still looking, or your child finding some favor with no real explanation? Sometimes, my friend, you just can't count the blessings because they are not visible. One example is good health, with soundness of mind and spirit.

If you are in perfect health, you may not look at that as a blessing, but it is. If your house is paid off, that's a blessing. You may say, "I worked and paid for this house," and that you did, my friend, but it was because of God's blessings you were able to do it.

Blessings don't follow simple math. Two plus two does not always equal four when dealing with God's blessing. Sometimes you may come up with a six, an eight, or even twelve. Remember the lad with his lunch of two fish and five barley loaves that fed over five thousand men, not counting women and children?

As evening approached, the disciples came to him and said, "This is a remote place, and it's already getting late. Send the crowds away, so they can go to the villages and buy themselves some food." Jesus replied, "They do not need to go away. You give them something to eat." "We have here only five loaves of bread and two fish," they answered. "Bring them here to me," he said. And he directed the people to sit down on the grass. Taking the five loaves and the two fish and looking up to heaven, he gave thanks and broke the loaves. Then he gave them to the disciples, and the disciples gave them to the people. They all ate and were satisfied, and the disciples picked up twelve basketfuls of broken pieces that were left over. The number of those who ate was about five thousand men, besides women and children.

Matthew 14:15–21

On a more personal note, my mother had no idea that four of her children would finish college; after all, neither she nor my father had completed high school. That math just doesn't make sense in the flesh. God's word tells us, time after time, that Jehovah can intervene in our lives, just to let us know how special we are to God, how great God is, and that we are only God's vessel.

But, using Biblical teaching and the application of faith, Christian Economics makes a lot of sense. We have talked about the mustard seed and the two fish and five barley loaves. Another example is the widow and her oil:

The wife of a man from the company of the prophets cried out to Elisha, "Your servant my husband is dead, and you know that he revered the LORD. But now his creditor is coming to take my two boys as his slaves." Elisha replied to her, "How can I help you? Tell me, what do you have in your house?" "Your servant has nothing there at all," she said, "except a little oil." Elisha said, "Go around and ask all your neighbors for empty jars. Don't ask for just a few. Then go inside and shut the door behind you and your sons. Pour oil into all the jars, and as each is filled, put it to one side." She left him and afterward shut the door behind her and her sons. They brought the jars to her, and she kept pouring. When all the jars were full, she said to her son, "Bring me another one." But he replied, "There is not a jar left." Then the oil stopped flowing. She went and told the man of God, and he said, "Go, sell the oil and pay your debts. You and your sons can live on what is left."

2 Kings 4:1–7

Although we believe it, let's face it, things like the widow and her oil or the feeding of five thousand do not happen every day. So, what do we do? Well with prayer and fasting, there are ways that Christians can use Christian Economics to make a difference every day. But, we need to know and understand clearly what Christian Economics really is and is not.

Christian Economics, which is just another form of stewardship, has four important activities: prayer, fasting, faith, and praise. With these four spiritual tools, you are well on your way to a successful life of fulfillment.

I had a colleague who claimed that the LORD gave her a new vehicle. It was one of those fancy SUVs, just a beautiful piece of machinery. She said she was just driving down the street (in her old vehicle), and the spirit spoke to her and said, "Look, that is your new car."

She parked, got out of her car, walked into the dealership, claimed the vehicle, and, voila, her credit was approved. A few months later, she was going through a divorce because her husband was aggravated with her impulsive spending. God does not bless us that way, beloved. The God I serve will not bless you by putting you in debt, especially to the point of division that could be the cause of a divorce. My friend, this is clearly *not* Christian Economics.

But, when I watched my mother take a cabbage, some leftover turkey, and the cornmeal and make a full meal for herself and her six children, well, I believe this was a good example of Christian Economics.

Or when you hear of a poor farmer with third-grade education finance (without Sallie Mae) his son's college education, it causes one to become a believer in Christian Economics.

Christian Economics, or stewardship, is a way of life. Take the life that we have and place it in God's hands. Through prayer and fasting, we will manage to get more out of life than the average person. There is no mystery here, rather it is stewardship combined with faith that are two very potent ingredients in a Christian's lifestyle.

Looking closer at stewardship, I am reminded of something that the Reverend C says: "It is good practice for Christians to live *under* their means."

What I believe she means is that most of us have the tendency to live just above our means, in other words, spend a little more than what we have and we make up that difference by charging it or buying on time, which places us in financial bondage.

We have been brainwashed to believe we need debt to survive. Some actually believe debt is the only way to obtain big-ticket items. Many even go further by acting as if credit cards are another form of currency. It is as if these persons never learned that all they were doing was adding to their financial burden by paying interest on top of the cost of the item they purchased. As I listen to people talk about debt, there is very little concern, until it compounds into a large indebtedness that leads to a credit crisis. Practicing good stewardship can avoid all of that. You really don't have to be a victim of debt. Our first action should be to *live under our means*.

I traveled with Reverend C and her husband—Bishop John Richard Bryant, the senior bishop of the African Methodist Episcopal Church— abroad and saw firsthand how excessive our living standards are in America compared to other parts of the world. It was disturbing to see us having so much and others having so little. I am not advocating that we all live in American poverty, but some of us go to the extreme with our acquisitions. I sometimes drive through a neighborhood on a Saturday just to count the many garage sales. People have accumulated garage loads of items until they could do nothing but try to sell them to others.

I believe you know a person that has so much in their garage that they can't park their car in it. Now, my friend, something needs to be said about accumulating so much stuff.

When we visited other countries, particularly the islands, we noticed that, for the average family, all household goods could fit into our auto garages, with space left over. Now, we all want to enjoy our life, after all, we worked for the enjoyment of it all, right? Well, not so fast. God wants all of us to be happy and fulfilled. Some of us accumulate to the point of over indebtedness, which will take away our joy and fulfillment because we are overwhelmed by debt. Being overwhelmed by debt is not how God wants us to live.

Now, don't get me wrong, I love life in America, and I believe the bishop and Reverend C do as well, but what Reverend C was pointing out is that there is plenty of room for us to grow without enslaving ourselves in debt with things that we don't really need. Most of us cannot tithe to the LORD, who gave us everything we have, because our eyes rule our decision-making process (we will talk about this more when we get to the section called "Fasting"). We want, we want, and we want. But if we can manage to adopt what I call the 70/30 Theory or Way of Life, your life and future will have an excellent chance to be secure.

This is only one of Reverend C's examples of living under your means where you can control your spending and financial allocations, not just for the present, but you will see, for a very bright future as well. I am not saying that you should never use credit; there is a time and place for it. Student loans, mortgages, automobiles, and emergencies are examples of appropriate situations for using credit; however, you should really define emergencies so that you don't lose control.

For instance, vacations are not emergencies; going out to dinner should not ever qualify, not to mention a new dress, suit, or any clothing items. You should be able to pay cash for these items, or don't purchase them.

Now, I will use my charge card to purchases these items, but I pay the entire charge-card bill when I receive it; that way, I pay no interest.

Again, if I feel I can't pay the entire bill when I receive it, I will not purchase that item.

The key to a successful life is the adoption of this plan, self-control, and consistency in following it. This is where prayer and fasting come in:

10 Percent to God by Way of Tithing

Here I followed the example given to us in the Book of Genesis: I gave my tithes first. Was it easy? No, but with prayer and fasting, I began to adjust my life to want less and gain more. Initially, I had to give up a lot and had to fast and pray for the strength to sacrifice and learn to live without, which was not at all American. Within a five-year period, however, I found the credit-card lifestyle had caught up with my colleagues who charged everything and were, therefore, in debt.

10 Percent to God's Servant

You are God's servant. Whether through an IRA or other forms of saving for the future, independent of Social Security or any pension plan, this concept will benefit you. This plan will help you build a foundation for the remainder of your life. You will find that if you set aside 10 percent of your discretionary income on a consistent basis, it will replace itself in ten years.

Do the math. If you save 10 percent of your income in an area of, let's say, 7 percent return with a 3 percent inflation, it will generate the same amount of money as you put in by itself within a ten-year period. But, if you continue, you will eventually replace your entire income. The key, however, is self-discipline, which you can only get by prayer and fasting.

10 Percent for Emergencies and Vacations

This is the most dangerous area because it is very challenging for Americans to determine what is considered an emergency. I played a game with myself and did not allow myself a vacation until my emergency funds exceeded one year in resources. I did not take a vacation until my 10 percent emergency fund doubled (two years' worth of resources), and then I allowed myself to use the excess for vacation. The key here is to never finance or charge vacations. If emergencies come, well, I have the means of meeting it. After I perfected this method, I found myself using the excess money for more savings and offerings because I really did not need as much money for vacations. Why? Because, through self-discipline, I learned how to plan good inexpensive vacations that were quite gratifying to my family and me.

70 Percent Budgeted for Living Expenses

This is also a challenging part of budgeting because, again, some of us (including me) have a difficult time determining what is a need and what is a want. We all know that we budget our needs, and with the excess, we determine which of our wants we can enjoy. Again, I played a game with myself. I did not allow wants to exceed 20 percent of my total budget. If I had the money, I would deny myself and place it in my emergency fund.

In my younger days, I would get a part-time job to fund my tithes and future funds because I always wanted a plush retirement life. I have a slight confession to make here. I kept part-time jobs, which were blessings for me, because I never budgeted my part-time monies, so part-time income was also a plus for me.

Yes, I learned that method from my big brother, who never ran out of money. However, I have to be truthful, he rarely spent it either.

This is what living under your means is. Trust me, if executed correctly, your period of inconvenience will last five years, tops. Of course, with a large family and low income, it may take longer, but this method can eventually work for everyone. If you are already in a lot of debt, it will slow you down but will not break you. The key to your success is planning and executing self-discipline.

This is why contributing to God's servant (you) is important. If a twenty-five-year-old person makes just $20,000 per year, with an annual increase of 3 percent (which is also the average annual rate of inflation, so the wages are really not increasing) and that person invests 10 percent of their income consistently with a rate of return of 7 percent (the banks have a historical average of 3 percent, and Wall Street has an average of 11 percent; therefore, we allow for an average of about 7 percent) and the person consistently contributes that 10 percent until they reach retirement at the following ages, the scenario will have these results:

AGE OF WITHDRAWAL	YEAR IN PORTFOLIO (THE PLAN)	"WORTH"	MONTHLY INCOME FOR LIFE WITHOUT AFFECTING THE PRINCIPLE
45	20	$80,00	$300
50	25	$120,000	$550
55	30	$200,000	$950
60	35	$300,000	$1,500
65	40	$430,000	$2,000
70	45	$600,000	$3,500

Note: Consult your financial planner or any financial professional of your choosing.

Can you use an extra $2,000 per month of income at retirement? Even if you start late, at age forty-five, you could have an extra $300 to 500 per month for the rest of your life, without touching the principle, so there will be monies for your heirs. Mind you, this is extra money, added to your Social Security, pension, or whatever is planned for you at your retirement. Do the math for yourself, and check my math with a financial planner. Don't take my word or anyone's word for it, verify the figures for yourself. You will find that time and consistency can make a world of difference in your finances. Don't let someone else dictate how you will be living at retirement. This is up to you. Go see a financial planner and take charge of your own life, starting today.

By the way, many of us take the approach to do nothing by making the excuse, "Well, I might not live that long." Indeed, you may not. But, statistics tell us that we are living longer.

So why not plan to live longer and better with more financial resources to make your retirement living as comfortable as possible? I am disturbed when I hear of retirees having to decide whether to pay for medication or buy food. I do not want that for you, beloved, and I am a firm believer that a little planning and self-control can give you an upper hand in your financial future. But it will not come to you like "manna from on high" came to the Israelites in the wilderness. You need to play a role in this by learning more about your financial options. The good news is that most Americans *do have options*. One option we have, right in front of us, is debt and the challenge of eliminating it. You probably will agree with me that debt is a noose on our neck.

The rich rule over the poor, and the borrower is
servant to the lender.

Proverbs 22:7

One of the pitfalls of America life is credit. But, as you can see, this is not unique to America or the capitalistic system. Unfortunately, credit has been around for quite a while. Why? Because self-discipline or delayed gratification is one of the most difficult things to master when we are surrounded with such good, attractive *toys*. Satan always knows how to make things look good to the eyes and feel good to the flesh. We find ourselves wanting it, and wanting it now.

Even if we can do without it completely, even if we reason with ourselves, we know that we can do without it, but there is something that tells us, "You deserve it," "You look so good with it," and, after all, "This is why you work." This is all satanic verbiage, and if we don't have a strong spirit of self-discipline, we will buckle under.

According to *The American Debt Adviser*, "If you're currently in a financial situation that you're finding hard to manage, you're not alone.

Americans have, on average, a half-dozen credit cards and nearly $10,000 in debt balances, not counting their mortgage." This figure is growing rapidly, thanks to high interest rates combined with insufficient income to pay it down. Credit-card interest rates range between 7 and 21 percent, depending on your credit score and institution. But, if we take an average of 14 percent (which is pretty conservative); the average person is paying $1,400 in interest if they pay the minimum amount recommended by their creditors, which is financially lethal to their pocket book. Using straight and simple uncompounded math means the average person is paying pretty close to $120 per month, just for the privilege of have something that they probably could have done without. This represents about half of that retirement plan we were talking about earlier.

So, if you can manage to stay out of debt, you can fund over 50 percent of your retirement plan, according our model above, and not change your lifestyle at all. Some people pay as high as 30 percent interest on charge cards if they have a bad credit score. This could literally double your payout. So, if you can avoid the interest, it could result in a $1,800 to $2,000 surplus per year in your discretionary funds, which means it could finance your entire future without changing one bit of your lifestyle. Just eliminating interest could make a world of difference in your life.

Avoid Debt at All Cost

- The average American will pay for their home three times before the mortgage is satisfied.

- It takes an average of seven years to pay off an item on a charge card if you just pay the minimum payment on an account that charges 7 percent interest.

- But, if you pay just the minimum payment as recommended by your creditors, with more than 13 percent interest (which is about the average) on that card, you will pay five times your original charge for ten-plus years before your balance is paid off.

- You can pay twice the amount for your car if you finance it at the offered rate of 7 percent for seventy-two months. By the way, leasing can be just as bad; you really need to read the fine print.

- Some charge-card companies will levy a $30 late-payment fee, regardless of your balance or credit standings with them.

- Some charge-card companies will levy a $30 fee if you charge more than your credit limit; they may not deny your purchase just to charge you that fee.

- Learn how compound interest works and how to calculate it yourself; it can be a real eye-opener.

All these are little tricks are legal and are written right in your consumer's contract that you sign when you first apply for your credit card. If you don't know all the pitfalls, they will jump up and bite you.

I would like you to consider the following pledge to adopt in your life. No, it is not meant to make you a monk or vow a life of poverty, but it is designed for you to have life and have it more abundantly—just not all at one time. It is designed for you to gradually become a good steward of your finances and life:

Pledge to Yourself and Be Determined To:

- Budget your finances using the 70/30 way of life. *Learn to live under your means.*

- Never put furniture, clothes, vacation, or personal items on a charge card or charge account, unless you pay the complete bill when it's due. Now, if you have a balance, we will talk later about how you can eliminate that balance.

- Pay off your credit cards in full each month, or cut the cards up. Sometimes, I look at charge cards as a vehicle of

Satan. If I cannot control it, I will cut it off and cast it into the fire, just like a branch that does not bear good fruit.

- Pay all debts you created. Never voluntarily file for bankruptcy because of your debt, unless it is the result of some catastrophic life illness or unemployment, for God understands that. But, filing for bankruptcy just to get out of debt is another form of stealing. But, if there is no other way out, go ahead, but be determined not to pass that way again.

- Acknowledge that God wants you out of debt. God calls us to peace. You cannot enjoy the full blessings of God when you are worried about debt or the debtors.

- Never stop tithing. Remember that to stop tithing is to tell God you can do it all without HIS help.

- Set a goal to give to the poor. Giving to charity is the quickest way to riches for yourself. When you allow the LORD to use you as HIS vehicle of blessing, you can't help but to be blessed.

- Have confidence that God will perform HER promises. If you stay connected to the vine and the husbandman, you will be blessed and empowered to do great things, just as Jesus taught in John 14.

- Avoid personal and business associations with dishonest people. You have heard the saying "Birds of a feather flock together." Don't flock with dishonesty; it may rub off on you. Get away from it, and purify yourself. After all, you are sanctified, purified, and filled with the Holy Ghost as a Christian, so don't pollute your spirit, because the Holy Spirit cannot deal in an unclean vessel.

- Do an honest day's work for an honest day's pay. Make yourself valuable to your employer. Look for additional ways to help your employer become successful. Don't worry; it always wears off on you. My mom always told us go into work about fifteen minutes earlier and leave about fifteen minutes later. Don't worry if the boss gives you something to do, do it, for it pays big dividends in the end.

- Set your goal to have a surplus account, cast it out, and claim it; it will happen, and when it does, learn what to do with it. Get away from thinking investing is a form of gambling. Investment is what makes this country and world run. Get a piece of the pie; learn how to invest to your level of comfort. The key to any financially successful person is to have your money work for you. This is not impossible, it's very tangible, but we will talk more about investments later.

- Maintain a good reputation and pay your bills. This adds to the integrity of the Christian. This is not just in paying bills—be a man or woman of your word. Signing a contract means you are making a commitment. You are giving your word to perform your part of the bargain. To not do what you gave your word to do is not integrity, it is dishonest. So, work on meaning what you say and saying what you mean. Always be honest with friends and coworkers. If you are in a position of authority, be honest with your employees and look out for their interest. Do what you can to promote those around you. That practice will pay you some pretty good dividends.

- Always maintain a good credit score. Check your score, for you never know when you may need to finance for emergencies. One way of maintaining good credit is always paying off your bills. Now, I agree, your score will not increase as fast when you pay off your balance early or all in one billing, but you will still have a good score if you continue that practice.

- Examine your home, assets, liabilities, and business to see if you are in a sure position, practicing at least an 80/20, if not 70/30, budget system.

- Eliminate your debt. This may seem far-fetched at the moment, but this should be your goal, and it is very possible, but we need to talk more about this later.

- Count the cost of any acquisition or purchase, and refuse to make hasty decisions, especially where debt or investments are involved.

- Acknowledge that God is the giver of all good and blessed things and that you are the custodian of his blessings. The better custodian you are, the more God will trust you.

- Don't be influenced by TV and computer advertisements. If you see yourself weakening, turn it off. Understand the goal of an advertisement: it is designed to convince you that you are better off with their item or service. In most cases, you are not better off.

Eliminating Debt

I talk a lot about eliminating debt because I believe that it is the one area of our lives in which Satan has been very successful. If Satan can get us to become miserable in our lives, he knows that others will find it hard to want to be Christians. After all, what have we to offer if we are going through the same misery as everyone else? But, if we can show that we mastered control and are living a life that is worry-free and even grows financially because we have become more effective stewards of our financial affairs, well, we can get an audience for that. Right?

So, the first thing we need to do is establish a method of reducing and eventually totally eliminating our debt. I can already hear you thinking, "He is really crazy."

But it is possible to live in America without debt and not be considered rich or wealthy even though I believe it is the first step in enjoying a truly rich life. Notice here, I am saying without debt, not without credit. Because of our capitalist system, everyone needs established credit, but that is entirely different than having debt, which is money you owe after replenishing your disposable income.

You need to promise yourself, with conviction, that you deserve the life that God wants for you: to be free of debt. Now, we discussed the four items that you probably need to finance: mortgage for a home, an automobile (which we plan to eliminate eventually), student loans, and emergencies, such as medical bills. Therefore, all other purchases and acquisitions should be off your list. From now on, you will not finance anything but items that fall into those four areas.

- First step: although most financial professionals will tell you to target the account with the highest interest rate, I have found physiological triumphs are far more effective. So, I want you to list all of your accounts in the order of balances, with the lowest balance being first on your list. I believe you will feel better and gain enthusiasm when you pay off your first bill and note how much interest you save at this point.

- Second step: determine the minimum payment of that account. Whatever it is, you need to create additional funds that will at least *double* that payment. The key is to continue paying at least that double amount until that bill is paid off. Create a deliberate surplus plan outside of your current budget and without cheating God by withdrawing your tithes. This could be the most difficult task because most of us do not have any surplus; that's why we have this dilemma. But, believe it or not, you can find surplus. You may need to eliminate a night out or a dessert for the week, but you can find a surplus somewhere. When I began this method, I got a part-time job that more than doubled my payments. This would be hard nowadays, especially if you have a family, but what's hardest is continuing to live under the yoke of debt, so find your way.

- Third step: once that bill is paid, identify your next target account and celebrate on it. How do you celebrate? Well, make your last charge on that account by maybe going out to dinner. But, while you are at dinner, you literally tear up the card of the first account to avoid charging on that account again.

- Fourth step: combine all of the payments on the first account, and add the amount to the second account you just targeted. For instance, if your first target account had a minimum payment of $30 and you doubled it to $60, it made your previous target payment $60. If your minimum payment of this second account is $30, then your new target payment will be $90. This is where you need to recommend to yourself to get completely out of debt because your mind will start to wonder, "Why am I doing this? I can buy...Or do..." But stick to it, because there's a big light waiting for you at the end of the tunnel. *Remember, do not buy or add to your debt.*

- Fifth step: once you have paid off the second charge account, you should be feeling pretty good. It's time to celebrate and destroy the second card. You may have a question about how many cards you destroy before you create another problem for yourself, like a lack of credit. Well, you should keep eliminating cards until you have two left. They will happen to be the two with the largest amount of credit anyway. It's probably good to have a MasterCard and a Visa.

With all honestly, it probably will take you a few years to pay off all of your credit-card debt using this method unless you can get a part-time job to speed up the process. If you do, please deny yourself, do not allow yourself to do anything with that part-time job income but pay off debt. But, any form of surplus income will really make a big difference.

It doesn't have to be a job, it could be a periodical chore for someone, or, as I mentioned earlier, eliminate a night out or reduce your vacation distance. It sounds tough, but, believe me; it's not as tough as living in debt or ending up in bankruptcy.

The other benefit in this method is that you are creating surplus to invest in your future, as well as increasing your lifestyle by eliminating your debt, because, after all is said and done, you won't be paying the Godforsaken interest and add-on fees, you will be free.

Continue to remind yourself that:

"God wants you out of debt."

Learn what it means to be in a surety position, and then don't allow yourself to be trapped in debt again. How can you do that? Remember the saying of Reverend C: "Learn to live *under* your means."

I know what it is to be in need, and I know what it is to have plenty. I have learned the secret of being content in any and every situation, whether living in plenty or in want. I can do everything through HIM who gives me strength.

Philippians 4:12–13

At times you need to keep up with the Joneses. You remember the saying "keeping up with the Joneses." It occurs when people make decisions based on what they think the Joneses have. However, being a good steward will turn the light on you. When people see that you are happy and not a victim of the debt crunch, they are going to wonder why. Because you will not appear to have any less than they have (and you won't), it will be a good evangelistic moment to show how good God has been to you by blessing you with the wisdom of stewardship.

I never worried about what somebody else had, and you should not either. If my neighbor buys a Cadillac every year, I will just say good for him, he's the one who has to pay for it. The scripture tells me that I should be just as content with my three- or ten-year-old Ford as long as it's paid for and operating properly. Through prayer and fasting, I learned and developed an attitude that I didn't need the latest fashion-designer suit or clothing as long as I was neat, clean, and presentable. Once I got past the fashions and the who's who, I was well on my way to living out Philippians 4.

But, you also need to know your comfort zone. Not everyone can fast or do without certain items because of their health, family members, and other factors that may not have anything to do with their willingness to fast or practice self-denial. As a father, I may not fast as much as I did as a single man. As a mother, you are willing to change certain living conditions for the sake of your family. So, your comfort zone may vary based on your life situation at the time. But, whatever your situation is, you should be able to find your comfort zone through good stewardship.

Don't outlive your lifestyle. Make an inventory of your finances and where you would like to be on a consistent basis. Don't live on the level you cannot afford yet. Remember, all that glitters ain't necessarily gold, and all that's big is not always best. If you long for a higher lifestyle, ask yourself why. Is it that people on that level look happier? Is it that you are impressed with the glamour or the bling? Well, think again. Is it worth you being in debt because you are living higher than what your resources can obtain for you? Ask God to help you adjust until you can do better.

Ask Jehovah to help you see what SHE has in store for you, and, most of all, what is best for you. It's not that God wants you to be poor, but many of us are where we are because of choices that we made previously. Did we finish school? Did we pursue our education and prepare the way we should have? Did we start a family too early or jump out in the deep too soon? Or are we still making decision that is not good for us?

Again, prayer and fasting can help us in this area. Many Christian believe all they need is to go to church and an occasional Bible study, and things should be all right. But, we need to be connected to the vine; we need to be able to produce for God.

Once we become the vine that produces good fruit, we then can produce for ourselves. Remember, "Seek first the kingdom of God, and these things will be given to you as well." When you seek to please God first and fast and pray for directions, you will develop a sense of contentment, and you will find luxury desires outside of your financial realm will start to diminish.

A good rule to remember: "If you have to finance it, it's out of your range." And if it's out of your range, that's a signal that you are moving out of your Stewardship Zone. I have another saying: "If it ain't in your pocket, leave it on the shelf." That does not mean you have to pay cash for everything you purchase, but it does mean that you should have the money in the checking account for your monthly bill so that you can write a check for the entire purchase.

There is another test that qualifies for the Stewardship Zone: that the zone or area we live in is well managed. This does not mean we are rich, but it does mean we are managing what we have and not stretching beyond our means. I had a conversation with my nephew Sean, who informed me that many define middle class as those who spend more than they earn or take in. Well, I don't think this is a definition of a group of people; rather it is a mind-set that is very productive for business in our capitalist society, because it accelerates sales and profits.

But it is also very dangerous to individuals, because using credit beyond their means gives them a false sense of success by accumulating items or stuff at the expense of interest, which eventually overwhelms them if it's not put in check.

There's an old Chinese proverb that says:

"A man who feels he has all he needs has just become rich."

So, my friend, my advice to you is to:

"Get out, and stay out, of debt."

Reactive Article

I work with my clients to design a personal financial plan based on their life goals. This strategy focuses on helping them become more confident about managing their financial objectives. It is designed to provide solutions to everyday and long-term financial questions and is personalized to meet the needs of high–net worth individuals and small-business owners.

Economics
Overview and Perspectives.
The author writes this chapter in a caring way, with the ministering spirit of a long-serving pastor, approaching the topic of money and capitalism in the real world with compassion and insightfulness.

First the chapter addresses certain financial myths in the Christian community and then, links Biblical scripture to sound, fundamental principles about money and personal finances.

Key illusions that are debunked are the notions that money is a panacea to happiness, fame, and personal problem resolution and that devout Christians can rely on miraculous, divine intervention to rectify their financial woes. Particular insight is provided to alter the thinking by Christians that principles of spirituality and personal-wealth building are at odds or serve counter-purposes.

What seems to work well is the carefully crafted way the reader is presented with a Biblical guide to prosperity through scripture, as well as a practical interpretation and translation of that scriptural context.

Overall, the basic building blocks to getting your financial house in order are addressed in both scripture reference and everyday practical terms (practice). Out-of-control finances, overwhelming indebtedness, and obsessing over money and materialism are not sound Biblical principles. Sound money management principles—such as becoming better savers, practicing first-fruits tithing, implementing household budgeting, and saving residual dollars for emergencies or retirement—are conducive to sound Christian Economics.

CONTROL YOUR CREDIT
(Credit is Satan's Spider web)

Chapter Four
Overview and Perspectives.

The author is not a pioneer in setting out passages of scripture intended to guide Christian believers to prosperity. Chapter Four addresses a major obstacle to financial self-determination: mismanaging credit. Even the basic steps towards financial prosperity are stifled (opening savings and checking accounts), if not totally defeated, by abuse of credit, according to the author. Comprehensive financial planning practiced in the secular world often delegates a client's debt issues to others with special expertise in the field. This chapter recites scripture and then links scripture to real-life action steps that can positively impact dysfunctional finances and poor habits for handling personal credit, personal borrowing, and credit-card usage.

The Christian tenets of building relationships with people who are honest in their personal and business dealings, who live ethical lifestyles, and who, in managing their household budgets, live within their means are referenced as habits of being good stewards of their finances. But everyday financial awareness and attention to avoiding impulse buying on credit, adopting a philosophy that unnecessary items are paid for in cash only or not purchased seem simple to implement yet dramatically effective. The chapter tries to keep its financial solutions within the reach of practical living habits that can be easily applied.

Kudos to the author for tackling the complex subjects of debt, credit, and liability management. As a spiritual guide to financial self-help, this chapter has to overcome considerable amounts of fiction and folklore related to financial planning in general and in interpreting passages of scripture to arrive at the truth about Christians and their finances. Laying out the mechanics of how to improve your FICO credit scores, how to accelerate getting out of debt, and the merits of living below your means could easily fill more than one chapter of this or any book on the subject. Addressing the issue of credit, in a Christian context and condensed to just a single chapter, is inspired reading.

David E. Cox, CFP
Financial Advisor
Troy, Michigan

Reactive Article

This subject is quite often avoided by single individuals, families, and entrepreneurs. Chapter Four provides assistance on the subject of successfully changing and starting habits to build a strong financial foundation to claim our inheritance.

After reading *Claiming Your Inheritance*, focusing on Chapter Four's economics, it reminded me of our mantra at the Small Business Development Center. In the center, we counseled entrepreneurs starting a business, and one of our first questions was, if you were building a house, would you begin construction without a blueprint? The response is no. Our mantra is to begin your business on a strong foundation, which is to develop a business plan—the small-business blueprint for success.

Small business owners often fall into the mind-set identified in this chapter. The mind-set is that only money can solve all problems in business, however, just as the author indicated, money alone is not the cure-all for obstacles that are caused by lack of management resources. We are encouraged to establish goals for the future and properly utilize the resources we are provided. The spiritual aspect of this chapter is both on point and relevant to entrepreneurs. Quite often, when we start a venture, it is undercapitalized. Capital becomes the guiding focus for the business instead of the initial goal of providing quality services in your field of expertise. Money alone is never the answer what we do and expect to do with the resources we have. Chapter Four lays out this aspect in a manner that is both spiritual and relevant to the subject. The spiritual aspects indicate to stand fast and trust that the work we have put in business planning and development is and will prevail over the hurdles that are inherent in starting and being successful in our ventures.

Lynda Garrison-Carlton
Certified Public Accountant
Carlton Accounting Service, Inc.
Naperville, IL
Telephone: 630-499-1886
E-mail: Lyndagc@aol.com

CHAPTER FIVE

RESILIENCE

Don't Quit

Resilience is a word that refers to strength and durability. Often used to describe materials, it is also used to describe a human response. In psychology, one often refers to the term "ego resilience," which is used to describe a "person's ability to respond adaptively and resourcefully to new situations," according to the book *Human Development: A Life-Span View* by Robert V. Kail and John C. Cavanaugh. In other words, the person is able to cope with stress and/or adversity. The person is able to return to normal functioning despite the experience or exposure that created the stress. Kail and Cavanaugh also state that, in studies of children who were thought to have high ratings of ego resilience, it was found that they were flexible in response to novel and changing social situations. Adults with high resilience demonstrated the ability to see opportunities for change. On the other hand, those with low resilience became frozen in place or experienced decline in function. The highly resilient person may also experience a temporary decline but then rebounds. We see these effects as we face critical life transitions (like a child entering junior high school or an adult facing a job loss during middle age).

While the psychological description of resilience sheds some light on how we respond to life's happenings, there is, I believe, a spiritual component or approach as well. I believe that the spiritual approach to facing life's crises has much to offer.

I remember listening to a sermon by the Reverend Nicholas Hood Jr., a pastor and city councilman in Detroit. Reverend Hood preached a sermon entitled "Never Quite," using the parable of the "Persistent Widow" appearing in the Book of Luke as a text.

Then Jesus told his disciples a parable to show them that they should always pray and not give up. He said: in a certain town there was a judge who neither feared God nor cared about men. And there was a widow in that town who kept coming to him with the plea, "Grant me justice against my adversary." For some time he refused, but finally he said to himself, "Even though I don't fear God or care about men, yet because this widow keeps bothering me, I will see that she gets justice, so that she won't eventually wear me out with her coming!"

Luke 18:1–5

Reverend Hood expounded on the text by reminding us, like that widow, sometimes we don't see a way out. We may need help from some pretty unpopular sources, but God will always make a way for us if we don't give up on ourselves. The widow in the parable continued to pray, fast, and exercise her faith. She did not sit at home with a woe-is-me attitude; rather she arose every morning and went forward, expecting a response, which she eventually received.

Most of the time, all we need to do is trust in God and trust in ourselves to the point that we put our trust into action by exercising our faith. Faith, as we discussed earlier, is an action word, not just something that we believe God can do but what we believe we can do by the empowerment of God's Holy Spirit working in and through us. Things will not always be easy, and some things will knock us back to the point where our goal may appear to be out of reach. But, God specializes in managing the things that seem impossible.

The good reverend encouraged his listeners to always strive and reach for the goal. He said that defeat is just a retreat for the winner. He proclaimed that we should all have a winner's attitude, knowing that "if I just keep striving, keep trying, keep praying, keep trusting, keep getting up, and keep trusting, I will make it." What a wonderful and powerful sermon that was, and I still remember it, although I heard it over twenty years ago. He ended his sermon with a poem entitled "Don't Quit" by an unknown author.

When things go wrong, as they sometimes will,
When the road you're trudging seems all uphill,
When the funds are low and the debts are high,
And you want to smile, but you have to sigh,
When care is pressing you down a bit,
Rest, if you must, but don't you quit.
Life is queer with its twists and turns,
As every one of us sometimes learns,
And many a failure turns about,
When he might have won had he stuck it out;
Don't give up though the pace seems slow—
You may succeed with another blow.
Often the goal is nearer than
It seems to a faint and faltering man,
Often the struggler has given up,
When he might have captured the victor's cup,
And he learned too late when the night slipped down,
How close he was to the golden crown.
Success is failure turned inside out—
The silver tint of the clouds of doubt,
And you never can tell how close you are,
It may be near when it seems so far,
So stick to the fight when you're hardest hit—
It's when things seem worst that you must not quit.

So, my friend, I too want to remind you not to quit. Develop the attitude of a winner by adopting spiritual resiliency. Marvin Sapp put it into the words of his 2006 hit song "Never Would Have Made It."

I never
Chorus: Never would have made it
No, I never
Chorus: Never could have made it without you
I would have lost it all
But now I see that you were there for me
And I can say
Never would have made it
Never could have made it
Without you
I would have lost it all
But now I see that you were there for me
I am stronger
Chorus: I'm stronger
I am wiser
Chorus: I'm wiser
Now I'm better
Chorus: I'm better
So much better
Chorus: I'm better

Spiritual resiliency not only gives you the strength to endure, but it also builds spiritual character, strength, and maturity. You can develop your spiritual resiliency by adopting the spiritual disciplines identified below.

Prayer

Have you ever heard the phrase "prayer changes things?" Well, I grew up hearing that phrase over and over again. As a Christian in poverty, you are taught to lean on sources outside of yourself for your refuge. Christians have been criticized about this for years. I remember reading an article that claimed, "Christianity is for weak people who use God as a crutch." I, along with others, took exception to that statement. I became quite verbal when I heard anyone agreeing or using that statement. But then I read a letter written by Paul to the Corinthians, which included this statement:

That is why, for Christ's sake, I delight in weaknesses, in insults, in hardships, in persecutions, in difficulties. For when I am weak, then I am strong.

2 Corinthians 12:10

It made me think. As I looked back on the "crutch" statement, I realized that the person was correct, but not in the sense that they meant. We are all flesh and are, by nature, weak and subject to sin. We can give in to sin very easily, or we can use prayer to help us to gain spiritual strength to overcome sin. I would like to reintroduce the saying "prayer changes things" with a different word: "prayer changes *me*." You see, it is prayer that helps me overcome my weaknesses and gives me that extra push, the inspiration to go on a little while longer. Yes, I am weak, weak to sin, but when I find myself giving way to sin, I pray, and God gives me that extra push to overcome. We call the extra push GRACE.

Bishop Gregory Gerald McKinley Ingram has a saying: "Much prayer, much power; little prayer, little power; no prayer, no power." Prayer strengthens us, prayer empowers us, and prayer invokes the spirit in us.

Without prayer, we are weak. When we are weak, prayer is like that can of spinach that Popeye used to overcome Brutus. Prayer is what we need for spiritual strength—that divine second wind, that energy boost from on high. I agree, I am weak, and I need strength and power to help me in my weakest hour, and with prayer, I can overcome and gain the strength that I need to carry on. As my cousin Carolyn, who is an Evangelist, sometimes says: "God doesn't want your Pop-Tart prayer." God is seeking our earnest petition and praise when we commune with HIM.

Some of us never pray to connect with our creator or strengthen our walk; rather, we use prayer strictly to petition for what we need.

Don't get me wrong, we should ask God for what we need (and maybe sometimes want) in the name of our risen Christ as Jesus instructed in John 14, but that should not be the only time SHE hears from us. God probably feels the way you do when your children or relatives seem to only call you when they need something. Do you know the saying, "No news is good news?" If you don't hear from that relative, you know everything is all right with them.

Well, God wants a different relationship with us. I believe prayer is also a part of worship, it should not be something that we do quickly just to say our Lord's Prayer, neither should we pray just when we are in need. My cousin Carolyn also said, "God is not your personal Jenny!" Prayer is far more than that; it reconnects us with the power source that can change our outlook, our circumstance, our situation, and our lives. Prayer is that power source that can give us whatever we need to overcome challenges and be triumphant in whatever we do.

Fasting

Prayer and fasting have a lot to do with developing your spiritual resiliency. Prayer is that spiritual connections that one has with God to connect, reconnect, and even improve our relationship with Yahweh. It is the main method one will use to move from being acquainted with God to having a relationship with God. Fasting is when a believer recognizes the need to not only be closer to God but believe and understand the need to connect with the Deity to the point of being a vehicle for God's use. Fasting strengthens us to do God's will in our lives and take charge of our lives so that we can be used by God. However, the biggest benefit from fasting is our self-discipline. Fasting is going through a process of self-denial and self-discipline to the point of cleansing all of the junk of the world and spiritual garbage so that we can better tap into the Divine Resource that is available to us as we get a better grip on *the vine*.

The more we fast, the more we become aware of those empty bells and whistles of this world and how meaningless they are to our true happiness. Take a toddler, for example, you may buy them toys and all sort of gadgets to entertain themselves, but if you leave that child alone, you may find them entertaining themselves with the more inexpensive and common things. For example, I observed my toddler loving to make music with pots and pans.

Fasting is a process of self-denial that teaches you to deny the flesh and the physical so that the spiritual can dominate your thoughts and desires. I made reference to the Dalai Lama, inferring that true peace, true happiness, and true contentment come from within. Fasting helps you revalue things that facilitate your satisfaction and eventual happiness. So, as we master fasting, we strengthen our spiritual muscles and gain a better whole or total being.

We know that the law is spiritual; but I am unspiritual, sold as a slave to sin. I do not understand what I do. For what I want to do I do not do, but what I hate I do. And if I do what I do not want to do, I agree that the law is good. As it is, it is no longer I myself who do it, but it is sin living in me. I know that nothing good lives in me, that is, in my sinful nature. For I have desire to do what is good, but I cannot carry it out. For what I do is not good I want to do; no, the evil I do not want to do—this I keep on doing.

Romans 7:14–19

Although this scripture reads more like a tongue twister, what it is telling us is that we have two natures within us. Remember the poem I introduced you to earlier? It can also be used to explain the challenge we face each day of our lives:

I have two natures on my breast
One is foul, One is blessed
One I love, and the other I hate
But the one I feed will dominate

I believe we contently live with two spirits within us. Because we were born in sin, it is natural that we gravitate toward sin. But, Christians have gone through a spiritual rebirth by accepting Christ as our Savior, or ruler of our lives. We vow to live our lives according to his teachings, his way of life, and following his example that is recorded in scripture. By doing that, we take on another nature; which begins a battle of good and evil on a daily basis.

Fasting is spiritual exercise that keeps us strong enough to weather the spiritual storm of good and evil within us. The more we deny the flesh, which is by nature evil, the more we obtain that divine strength of a spiritual righteousness. Prayer and fasting feeds that spiritual nature that can only come from staying connected with the vine, our spiritual source.

I am the true vine, and my Father is the gardener. He cuts off every branch in me that bears no fruit, while every branch that does bear fruit he prunes so that it will be even more fruitful. You are already clean because of the word I have spoken to you. Remain in me, and I will remain in you. No branch can bear fruit by itself; it must remain in the vine. Neither can you bear fruit unless you remain in me. I am the vine; you are the branches. If a man remains in me and I in him, he will bear much fruit; apart from me you can do nothing. If anyone does not remain in me, he is like a branch that is thrown away and withers; such branches are picked up, thrown into the fire and burned. If you remain in me and my words remain in you, ask whatever you wish, and it will be given you. This is to my Father's glory, that you bear much fruit, showing yourselves to be my disciples.

John 15:1–8

Faith

We are about to enter an area that has confused many Christians. I, for one, went for years with the wrong definition of faith. I collected sayings about faith, such as, "Faith is not believing that God can, it is knowing that HE will." Well, now that I have matured, I have learned to say it a little differently: "Faith is not just believing that God can, it is knowing that HE will, through me." You see, now I am convinced that faith is more than just believing—it is putting your belief to action.

And a woman was there who had been subject to bleeding for twelve years, but no one could heal her. She came up behind him and touched the edge of his cloak, and immediately her bleeding stopped. "Who touched me?" Jesus asked. When they all denied it, Peter said, "Master, the people are crowding and pressing against you." But Jesus said, "Someone touched me; I know that power has gone out from me." Then the woman, seeing that she could not go unnoticed, came trembling and fell at his feet. In the presence of all the people, she told why she had touched him and how she has been instantly healed. Then he said to her, "Daughter, your faith has healed you. Go in peace."

Luke 8:43–48

Here, we see that faith can be so strong that it can produce power to heal. The woman was determined to be healed by Jesus. But, more than that, her belief took her to another level, a level of power production that actually became the healing force. Jesus was that focus point that triggered the event. Have you believed in something so strongly that you knew beyond the shadow of doubt that it had already happened; it just was waiting for you to claim it? Well, my friend that was the type of faith that this sister had. She knew that all she had to do was to get to the power source. She not only believed, she put her belief into action and moved, crawled, squeezed her way to claim her healing.

Another example of faith is the Blind Beggar:

As Jesus approached Jericho, a blind man was sitting by the road-side begging. When he heard the crowd going by, he asked what was happening. They told him, Jesus of Nazareth is passing by. He called out, "Jesus, Son of David, have mercy on me!" Those who led the way rebuked him and told him to be quiet, but he shouted all the more, "Son of David, have mercy on me!" Jesus stopped and ordered the man to be brought to him. When he came near, Jesus asked him, "What do you want me to do for you?" "Lord, I want to see," he replied. Jesus said to him, "Receive you sight; your faith has healed you." Immediately he received his sight and followed Jesus, praising God. When all the people saw it, they also praised God.

Luke 18:35–43

In both cases, those healed believed independent of public opinion or earthly circumstances. They did not care what people thought, and they did not care about people's reactions. As a matter of fact, their action appears to go against the norm, defying compliance and boldly taking charge of their quest for healing. Which brings me to my next point: when the blind man was healed, he and the people praised God.

Praise

You remember the story of the man who joined a very prestigious church in town. This was a pretty sophisticated congregation that had grown irritated with him because of his outbursts of praise at seemingly every Sunday worship service. The officers of the church, who, for the most part, were professional people, felt "it don't take all of that" to worship.

A couple of them decided to pay the old farmer a visit in an effort to warn him that if he continued his uncouth outbursts, they would request that he try another congregation. As they approached the old farmer's house, his wife opened the door to welcome them but informed them that he was out in the field in the back forty acres. Well, they weren't too keen on walking in the field, but they had made up in their minds to discuss this matter with him.

The elderly gentleman saw them coming and met them halfway with a wild and warm welcome. "Praise the Lord, my brothers! So glad to see you in the middle of the week. What brings you to my abode?"

Well, the head officer explained their mission and warned the gentlemen that if he could not control his emotions, they felt he might be more comfortable in another congregation. After all, they couldn't understand why he had to be so emotional. "Well, my brother," the old farmer said, "you see that woman who met you at the house? God led me to marry her some forty-plus years ago. God then blessed us with six wonderful children who didn't give us one ounce of trouble.

"That woman God gave me supported everything I wanted to do, and she reared my children to be upright and outstanding citizens. All are college graduates and doing very well for themselves. You see this land you are standing on? Well, God gave it to me through sharecropping as I was about to raise my family.

"Brother, when I think about all the wonderful things that God has done for me and my family, I can't help shouting and praising his Holy name. As a matter of fact, I feel myself getting excited right now; so, hold my mule while I SHOUT!"

God loves our praise. It's just another way of saying thank you to God or Halleluiah to the most high God. Remember the story of the Ten Healed of Leprosy?

Now on his way to Jerusalem, Jesus traveled along the border between Samaria and Galilee. As he was going into a village, ten men who had leprosy met him. They stood at a distance and called out in a loud voice, "Jesus, Master, have pity on us!" When he saw them, he said, "Go, show yourselves to the priests." And as they went, they were cleansed. One of them, when he saw he was healed, came back, praising God in a loud voice. He threw himself at Jesus' feet and thanked him—and he was a Samaritan. Jesus asked, "Were not all ten cleansed? Where are the other nine? Was no one found to return and give praise to God except this foreigner?" Then he said to him, "Rise and go; your faith has made you well."

Luke 17:11–19

Part of Christian Economics is the praise. We are taught that God loves praise. In the boldness of faith, we also should have the boldness of praise. Acknowledging God is required of us, especially when HE has done something for us. When I was a young lad, we could not eat without giving praise and prayer of thanksgiving; when rising in the morning, we were taught to give God the praise with a prayer of thanksgiving; and when we retired for the night, we must give God the praise with a prayer of thanksgiving. Our mom would demonstrate her thanksgiving at any time during the day by letting out "Praise the Lord!" All of this is Christian Economics, a lifestyle you adopt to survive. But, as I matured, I learned that the proper term for this is stewardship.

CHAPTER SIX

INTEGRITY
Doing the Right Thing

What is integrity? Wikipedia defines integrity as "the quality of being honest and having strong moral principles; moral uprightness. The state of being whole and undivided; adherence to moral and ethical principles; soundness of moral character." Others may look at integrity as the undiminished commitment to preserve the quality of what is right.

Some will argue, and I am one of them, that people have differing definitions of integrity, and its absolute meaning becomes nothing more than a poll of what is right, honest, and moral. All the descriptors of integrity—right, honest, and moral—have their own descriptions and meaning according to custom, culture, the day and age, and even ethnic group. What was right in our society fifty years ago may be frowned upon today. Back in the 1950s, it was right for us to raise our daughters to be whatever they wanted to be as long as they cooked, washed, cleaned the house, and were prepared to be a good mom and wife. It was considered irresponsible to train our daughters otherwise. Today, however, you would not dare take that approach without being regarded as a sexist. My mother did something quite unusual, yet tolerable, in rearing us: she trained her sons to do all homemaking chores as well.

We boys had to do all duties in house cleaning and had our own day to cook family meals, beginning at around age twelve. Each one of us developed a specialty of our own by age sixteen.

When I was growing up, the use of birth control pills was discussed and used by the wealthy, or those who could afford them. The rest of us looked at birth control pills as a sinful tool used only by sluts and perverts. After all, sex is only for when you are married. Now, even the church is promoting the pill and condoms. We, the church, however are still steadfast in maintaining our belief that abortion is wrong because it is a form of murder.

I remember growing up in a church that had a female minister who was shunned by most of the male clergy of that time. Now, however, we have female bishops among the various ministries of the church. Even the Roman Catholic Church is wrestling with the possibility of ordaining women just to survive. Why? Because women are just not taking that theology (which is not Biblically based) any more. How did all these changes happen? Was it women's liberation, Woodstock, or maybe the civil rights movement?

Really, my friend, it doesn't matter what triggered the changes; the fact is, change evolved and will continue to evolve because that's the nature of humanity. Therefore, what is right, honest, and moral, which are all components of integrity, is defined by our society and what seems to be the popular thing at the time we are living in. That's not a good way to measure integrity.

Unfortunately, changes will continue with the shifts in our society, which means our integrity is subject to change. This makes the very word integrity an oxymoron; that is, it presents us with incongruent or contradictory meanings.

Integrity is looked upon as something that is consistent, steadfast, and unwavering. Yet, if we look at what is right, honest, and moral, those things change, just as society changes.

Our president, for instance, changed his opinion on same-sex marriages, not because he himself believes in it but because of public opinion. But, what if I tell you that Christian Integrity does not change and is not subject to the Gallup poll?

I do not wish to insult your Biblical intelligence by presenting a few scriptures to reinforce my argument, but please allow me a few minutes of your time to share what I consider undisputed and unwavering Divine Instructions.

Let's start from the very beginning:

And God said, "Let the land produce living creatures according to their kinds: livestock, creatures that move along the ground, and wild animals, each according to its kind." And it was so. God made the wild animals according to their kinds, the livestock according to their kinds, and all the creatures that move along the ground according to their kinds. And God saw that it was good. Then God said, "Let us make man in our image, in our likeness, and let them rule over the fish of the sea and the birds of the air, over the livestock, over all the earth, and over all the creatures that move along the ground." So God created man in HIS own image. In the image of God HE created him; male and female HE created them. God blessed them and said to them, "Be fruitful and increase in numbers; fill the earth and subdue it. Rule over the fish of the sea and the birds of the air and over every living creature that moves on the ground."

Genesis 1:24–28

Now, I don't consider myself a fundamentalist, or a liberal for that matter, so I do not believe the Bible was written to be taken word for word. However, this passage of scripture seems to be very clear that the intent of God was to create humanity—male and female. HE, God, then told them, male and female, to "increase in number," which means to procreate or reproduce, have babies, become mommies and daddies. Beloved, I don't care how you try to slice that cake, it is still a cake. There is no place in God's plan of creation where Jehovah describes any other gender than male and female for this very reason. The differences are for the purpose of procreation.

Let's go a little further, shall we?

The two angels arrived at Sodom in the evening, and Lot was sitting in the gateway of the city. When he saw them, he got up to meet them and bowed down with his face to the ground. "My lords," he said, "please turn aside to your servant's house. You can wash your feet and spend the night and then go on your way early in the morning." "No," they answered, "we will spend the night in the square." But he insisted so strongly that they did go with him and entered his house. He prepared a meal for them, baking bread without yeast, and they ate. Before they had gone to bed, all the men from every part of the city Sodom—both young and old—surrounded the house. They called to Lot, "Where are the men who came to you tonight? Bring them out to us so that we can have sex with them." Lot went outside to meet them and shut the door behind him and said, "No, my friends. Don't do this wicked thing. Look, I have two daughters who have never slept with a man. Let me bring them out to you, and you can do what you like with them. But, don't do anything to these men, for they have come under the protection of my roof." "Get out of our way," they replied. And they said, "This fellow came here as an alien, and now he wants to play the judge! We'll treat you worse than them."

They kept bringing pressure on Lot and moved forward to break down the door. But the men inside reached out and pulled Lot back into the house and shut the door. Then they struck the men who were at the door of the house, young and old, with blindness so that they could not find the door. The two men said to Lot, "Do you have anyone else here—sons-in-law, sons or daughters, or anyone else in the city who belong to you? Get them out of here, because we are going to destroy this place. The outcry to the LORD against its people is so great that he has sent us to destroy it."

Genesis 19:1–13

Is that clear enough for you, beloved? God had no tolerance for homosexuality. I believe after reading this scripture that this is one area of sin where God may choose to react in a very harsh and mighty way.

Let's go further:

Do not lie with a man as one lies with a woman; that is detestable.

Leviticus 18:22

Now, you may say, "Preacher, this is all Old Testament stuff and does not apply to the New Covenant of Grace. Well my friend, we need to read a little further then:

For although they knew God, they neither glorified him as God nor gave thanks to him, but their thinking became futile and their foolish hearts were darkened. Although they claimed to be wise, they became fools and exchanged the glory of the immortal God for images made to look like mortal man and birds, animals and reptiles. Therefore God gave them over in the sinful desires of their hearts to sexual impurity for the degrading of their bodies with one another. They exchanged the truth of God for a lie, and worshiped and served created things rather than the Creator—who is forever praised. Amen. Because of this, God gave them over to shameful lusts. Even their women exchanged natural relations for unnatural ones. In the same way the men also abandoned natural relations with women and were inflamed with lust for one another. Men committed indecent acts with other men, and received in themselves the due penalty for their perversion.

Romans 1:21–27

Now, I feel it is my responsibility to clarify a few things. I am not suggesting that God has brought the HIV or AIDS viruses as a punishment on humanity because of homosexuality. Nor am I submitting reasons for hurricanes, tsunamis, earthquakes, or September 11th, as some of my colleagues have suggested as punishments for our sins. But I am saying the scripture warns us of this type of behavior.

God's response to that behavior is totally out of my league or line of teaching. My purpose is not to condemn but, rather, to explain God's word and intent. I also want to emphasize that God may hate the sin but loves the sinner, and that is good news for you and I. Why? Because, "By the grace of God, there go I."

To understand spiritual or Christian Integrity, I would like to share a definition from the Right Reverend John Richard Bryant, who said,

"It has been said that integrity is doing the right thing, even if nobody is watching...Stuart Matthews writes that essentially it is being true to yourself and in turn being the true 'you' to the world."

King David was not acting with integrity when he coveted Uriah's wife. Nor did he consider his spiritual integrity when he plotted the death of his fellow soldier to cover up his wrongdoing. Even his cry for forgiveness was not within the boundaries of integrity, for he only cried out to the LORD when Nathan, the prophet of God, brought David's scandalous deeds to his attention. Asking for forgiveness when your sins have been uncovered is a good thing to do, but it's not integrity. Asking for guidance away from sin regardless of how tempting it may be or whether you feel you won't get caught is integrity. Integrity may mean facing the music and ridicule of society for what is righteous and within the will of God.

Take Joseph, the son of Jacob, who walked in integrity when he rejected Potiphar's wife. Now notice, my friend, this was long before the Ten Commandments. There was no written Law then, only the person's willingness to walk with God and to be led by God's Spirit (yes, the Holy Spirit did exist in the Old Testament). He continued to walk in integrity even though it cost him prison time and abandonment. However, by living with integrity, Joseph was blessed beyond measure and given the glory of not only saving his family from famine but a nation of people for years to come.

For rulers hold no terror for those who do right, but for those who do wrong. Do you want to be free of fear of the one in authority? Then do what is right and he will commend you.

Romans 13:3

Remember Shadrach, Meshach, and Abednego, three Hebrews whose names were changed to serve the king, Nebuchadnezzar. They were required to bow down and worship a golden image whenever they heard the sound of the horn, flute, zither, or other instruments. When they were reported for disobeying the king's edict, they responded:

O Nebuchadnezzar, we do not need to defend ourselves before you in this matter. If we are thrown into the blazing furnace, the God we serve is able to save us from it. And he will rescue us from it, and he will rescue us from your hand, O king. But even if he does not, we want you to know, O king, that we will not serve your gods or worship the image of gold you have set up.

Daniel 3:16–18

Integrity is not only required when we are grandstanding on television or at a party, it is often required when we are in danger of losing friends, the approval of loved ones, and, yes, political votes. Integrity is doing the right thing, even when it appears that you are running this race alone and no one seems to understand. You see, beloved, popularity does not always dictate what is right. We have a guide, which is the Holy Scripture, that does not have all the answers, but it has enough for us to live a righteous life.

Now, no one is asking you to face a fiery furnace or to go to prison for standing up for what is right. Most of us will never be faced with these circumstances, so our cost would never be that high.

But the examples we have given should give you a picture of how serious we need to be in walking with integrity. Most of us will only be called names or may lose a friend or two in the process. For the most part, we will never be faced with a dilemma such as Shadrach, Meshach, Abednego, Daniel, or Joseph's, but we should be just as committed to integrity. In the absence of integrity, a mother will conspire with a son to lie to a father to steal another son's birthright; a brother will kill a brother; a brother will rape his own sister; disciples will betray a master; a mother will endanger her children; and fathers will desert families. Yes, without integrity, a four-day journey can take forty years, and a leader could never see the Promised Land.

In our own time, we have witnessed devastation that follows the absence of integrity. We have seen economic fallout on Wall Street, scandal after scandal hit public personalities and leaders in high places, ministries wiped out, and families ruined, all because of the absence of integrity.

Now, before you get the impression that I am against the president of the United States, please allow me to emphasize that I am clergy; I preach and teach spiritual integrity, but as president, he walks and talks the integrity of the people. As our political leader, he makes decisions that you and I probably cannot comprehend facing, let alone, wrestling with. I am very proud of him and what he has done for our country. As clergy, however, I take the place of Nathan and other prophets who try to remember the populous we are and to whom we belong and how we should live. Most of the decisions of our president have been overwhelmingly righteous, and I believe in the will of God, particularly in the areas of health care, confronting world terrorism, education, international treaties, and immigration, just to name a few. He has my vote. For after all is said and done, he is walking in integrity and doing the right thing.

The United States of America presents another form of an oxymoron. Imagine this: we are a country that was founded on religious freedom, and we claim to be a Christian society. Yet, we are constantly arguing religious matters. You cannot have religious freedom and say, "In God we trust." For, to say in God we trust, we are saying that we believe in God and we are following God's guidelines for living. But, on the other hand, demand that we have the freedom to do whatever we want.

When we deviate from God's word and God's guidelines, we are not a Christian society. By making this statement, I am assuming the guidelines are from the Holy Bible. But even that raises the question of which one? Are we referencing the Jerusalem Bible (Roman Catholic), the King James Version (Protestant), or the one Thomas Jefferson wrote as his version of the Bible? Or how about the Good News version, or even the Message Bible with very different versions, which raises serious questions by theologians who are very concerned with its use and references by laymen?

I was blessed by having God send me so many special people in my life. One was the Reverend Rudi Gelsey, a Unitarian Universalist pastor

I met in the 1980s. The good reverend published his own version of the Bible by abstracting all negatives, like violence, sexism, ethical differences, and division of cultures and nations. Reverend Gelsey entitled his publication *Imagine: A New Bible*. What a wonderful concept, what a wonderful approach to the God of love, peace, and harmony. Wouldn't that be a wonderful basis upon which to live our lives?

But, we will still have those who would argue the violence in the Bible is necessary, for it was part of the wrath of God, which was needed. Others would argue that sexism is needed to understand the role and functions of the sexes (oh really?). Don't forget the difference in cultures and nationalities, for God created a "chosen people," and we really need to know that.

So, the bottom line is: which Bible will we use as a basis for decisions? Now that was all for the Christian Community. What about the Israelites, Muslims, Hindus, and Buddhists, just to name a few? Now, we can't forget the Agnostics, even though we can exclude the Atheists because they aren't really human because they weren't created (don't take that literally).

Get the picture yet? Until we can agree on what religious freedom is in this country, we will always be plagued with this sometimes downright vicious argument of who is on the right side of God and who is walking in integrity. If we lived in a theocracy, all those arguments would go away. That is precisely what God wanted to do with the Israelites, but you probably know what happened there. Living in a democracy that is run on capitalistic principles presents us with a social oxymoron that will never be resolved.

I believe spiritual integrity takes us a step above all of that. I believe the God I serve has given us words to live by and a spirit with which to live. You see, that is why Joseph, the son of Jacob, walked in integrity before there even was a Ten Commandments or the Law, which are the guidelines for living a righteous life. Call it what you want to call it, but I choose to call it the HOLY SPIRIT, which I pray will walk with me and dwell within me so that I can walk, talk, and live in integrity.

CHAPTER SEVEN

TALENT

A Gift or a Curse

My favorite scripture, although I love many, is probably the parable of the Talents. You know the story.

Again, it will be like a man going on a journey, who called his servants and entrusted his property to them. To one he gave five talents of money, to another two talents, and to another one talent, each according to his ability. Then he went on his journey. The man who had received the five talents went at once and put his money to work and gained five more. So also, the one with the two talents gained two more. But the one who had received the one talent went off, dug a hole in the ground and hid his master's money. After a long time the master of those servants returned and settled accounts with them. The one who had received the five talents brought the other five. "Master," he said, "you entrusted me with five talents. See, I have gained five more." His master replied, "Well done, good and faithful servant! You have been faithful with a few things; I will put you in charge of many things. Come and share your master's happiness!" The servant with the two talents also came. "Master, you entrusted me with two talents; see, I have gained two more." The master replied, "Well done, good and faithful servant! You have been faithful with a few things; I will put you in charge of many things. Come and share your master's happiness!" Then the servant who had received one talent came. "Master, I knew that you are a hard man, harvesting where you have not sown and gathering where you have not scattered seed. So I was afraid and went out and hid your talent in the ground. See, here is what belongs to you." The master replied, "You wicked, lazy servant! So you knew that I harvest where I have not sown and gather where I have not scattered seed? Well then, you should have put my money on deposit with the bankers, so that when I returned I would have received it back with interest." "Take the talent from him and give to the one who has ten talents." For everyone who has will be given more, and he will have an abundance. Whoever does not have, even what he has will be taken from them. And throw that worthless servant outside, into the darkness, where there will be weeping and gnashing of teeth!

Matthew 25:14–30

I believe this parable is indicative of life and of God's expectation of each and every one of us. I believe God has given us a purpose, a calling, or you can say a mission. From creation or birth, Jehovah has given us the tools and equipment, which the scripture refers to as "talents" that we need to accomplish our goal or task here on earth, whatever it may be. Our challenge is to find out what our life's purpose is and devise a plan to execute our purpose by using the divine manual or guide book that our Creator has sent us, which is the Holy Bible. We are then to live out our purpose with the fuel, power, and ability Elohim has provided through the Holy Spirit, which empowers us, provided we learn how to tap into God's divine resources by exercising *stewardship*.

Getting back to our scripture of the talents, in order to fully understand the parable and why I believe it is so profound to us, we need to address a few key words and terminology in the passage.

Firstly, we need to understand a talent. Although our culture and English-language definition will work in this particular case, we really need to understand the Greek meaning of the word Talent that Christ used in his illustration. Talent actually means volume or measurement of weight in currency. A talent is equivalent to what was referred to as a unit of "one man's weight." This meant that it was the weight that an average man could carry. Most historians agreed this was about seventy-five pounds. Well, that counts me out on the carrying department. Nevertheless, it gives us the value one must have if they possess a talent of silver, gold, or anything of value. But, since our passage is taken from the Palestinian culture of 10–30 AD, we can safely assume it was silver. Therefore, a talent of money is considered to be seventy-five pounds of silver.

If we were to use the value of silver, using the date of this publication, which is about $10 per ounce (16 ounces per pound equals 1,200 ounces in one talent), this would make a talent of silver worth around $12,000. So, to the first servant, he would have given five talents of silver, or about $60,000, to the second servant about $24,000, and the third servant a measly $12,000 of his fortune. Well, the first servant invested that $60,000, although we don't know in what, but we do know he doubled his master's trust, resulting in approximately $120,000.

The second servant also put the money to work and also got a 100 percent return on his master's money. Although we don't know how long it took, the master seemed to be quite pleased when he returned to reconcile with them and hear the financial report of the first servant. Likewise, he heard and rejoiced at the financial report of the second servant, who delivered to his master double the money he was given.

However, the third servant began to make excuses. Most likely, the third servant had demonstrated fear and a lack of confidence, which is why the master probably did not trust him with much in the first place. Remember, the scripture said, "According to their ability or faith." That did not mean the servant could not produce, it only meant that the servant did not show the attitude or appearance of a good steward.

Well, my friend, we have embarked on that magic term—stewardship. And that is what this passage of scripture and this writing is all about: using what God has given us to gain favor from HIM, not to mention a little benefit for ourselves. But it is also important for us to remember this is *not a choice*. Stewardship is a requirement, an expectation, a mandate, and a charge. You cannot, and we are not to just sit on or bury the means God has given to us with which to produce. If we do, we are no better than the third servant who buried his talent. Can you imagine burying $12,000 in the ground? That act would be like an abomination where I came from. God has given to us all that we need to be successful and productive. Whether five, two, or one talent, our Creator expects us to use what is given to us and make something out of it.

So then, each of us will give an account of himself to God.

Romans 14:12

Try not to look at the amount given to you, my friend; whether a little or a lot, it still matters what you do with what you have been given.

But the one who does not know and does things deserving punishment will be beaten with few blows. From everyone who has been given much, much will be demanded; and from the one who has been entrusted with much, much more will be asked.

Luke 12:48

Allow me to point out another application of the Parable of the Talents. If we use our English definition of talent, we will find that it means that you possess a skill or ability to think or perform tasks that the average person finds difficult or just plain impossible to do, particularly the way you can. As we reflect on history or just the people we know, we can identify persons of talent. The Matthew passage implies that every servant (person) has some talent. I remember years ago, as a young lad, admiring some kids who seemed to have it all. They were talented in so many things, much like the servant who received five talents. Some persons were just good with one or two things, which seemed more than what I had at the time. Yet, in this very passage of scripture, I found a great deal of hope, even for me. You see, it gives me the impression that God gives each and every one of HIS servants something. It appears that all have the capability of doubling what they originally received. If my analysis is correct, it's saying that all of us have the ability and the potential to double our output and produce much more than that with which we began. Wow, that is some mighty good news, my friend. No matter how little we think we have, God has implanted in us the ability to produce much more, even from what we may conceive as small. No matter where I began, no matter what little I have, I can be great if I invest my God-given talent(s) and create a return for myself and my Creator.

But, I have to invest in myself, and I must have faith in myself, for if I apply Matthew 25:14–30 to my life, I will realize God has already given me what I need to succeed. The best part is that it does not matter what the other person has, what matters is our *faith*, not only in God that made us and already put what we need in us, in Christ that strengthens us, and the Holy Spirit that empowers us but also *ourselves*.

The servant that received one talent did not fail because he only had one talent. He failed because he did not work or use what he had. Yes, the servant was afraid, and, yes, he felt his lord did not earn what he had, but that appeared to be an excuse for his lack of faith. Many of us, including myself, have had those days, periods, and moments in our lives where we question our abilities and just gather excuses for our lack of motivation that really resulted in the failure. It is not that we do not have the resources, we just lack faith.

Let's examine *faith* for a moment. In order to do that, we need a good understanding of the word. Many of us learned that faith is believing God can do what we want HIM to do. Well, kinda, sorta. Faith is more than belief. You see, belief is like a hypothesis; it is a statement that we perceive as true, but with a hypothesis, one has to test it to prove it to be true before it can become fact. Once the hypothesis is tested to the point of what scientists call "universal acceptance" or "group approval," it then can be considered fact. In other words, a hypothesis rests on and is totally dependent upon the approval of others. I believe a chair will hold me. Following many tests, engineers have probable reasoning that, with the right dimensions, geometric design, and measurements and considering the material and construction, we would have statistical probability to reason that the chair should hold me.

But faith is when I put my belief to action. It is not until I actually exercise my faith and sit in the chair that my proof or testimonial results occur. In other words, faith is our belief put into action, no matter what the theory, study, test, or even universal belief is at the time. Remember, it was universal acceptance in Spain, in the fourteenth and fifteenth centuries, that the world was flat.

Christopher Columbus must have read Paul's Epistle when he sailed to Spain and all over Asia Minor without falling off the side of the earth, because he had enough evidence to convince the Queen to invest in his theory and approve his journey to the new world. We can reflect on many historical accomplishments that occurred after people said it was not possible. Many achievers were people who not only believed but also went a step further: they put their belief into action by exercising great faith in God and HER created vessel—themselves.

That poor servant with the one talent had one talent and one obstacle: himself. It was only one talent that he needed, but it was only one obstacle that stopped him from reaching his goal, also called *himself*. Beloved, this book is written to share one of the most profound mysteries and gift of God:

YOU

But if you don't have faith that God has given you all that you need to succeed, then you might as well put this book down and walk away, because it's all based on you believing that God loves you and me so much that SHE has given you and I this gift. You must have the faith to see it through, and without that faith, you will not be able to take advantage of the wonderful information contained in this book. Yes, many will call you a dreamer or down right crazy because your vision may be beyond the scope of the norm. If we all just thought from within the box, our society would not celebrate innovators like Alexander Graham Bell and his assistant who gave us the telephone. Without belief beyond common thought, we would not know of the Wright brothers, and it would still take days to travel by road or sea rather than a few hours in flight.

Without the dreams and beliefs of Dr. Charles Drew, many would have died without blood plasma. The world of technology would have evolved much slower without Steve Jobs.

There is another twist to talents or God's gift that I would like to bring out. It's found in the Gospel of Luke, Chapter 12, where the Christ tells a parable of the Rich Fool:

Someone in the crowd said to him, "Teacher, tell my brother to divide the inheritance with me." Jesus replied, "Man who appointed me a judge or an arbiter between you?" Then he said to them, "Watch out! Be on your guard against all kinds of greed; a man's life does not consist in the abundance of his possessions." And he told them this parable: "The ground of a certain rich man produced a good crop. He thought to himself, 'What shall I do? I have no place to store my crops.' Then he said, 'This is what I'll do. I will tear down my barns and build bigger ones, and there I will store my grain and my goods. And I'll say to myself, "You have plenty of good things laid up for many years. Take life easy, eat, drink, and be merry."' But God said to him, 'You fool! This very night your life will be demanded from you. Then who will get what you have prepared for yourself?' This is how it will be with anyone who stores up things for himself but is not rich toward God.

Luke 12:16–21

Here we find a warning about how we look at and use our talents or blessings from God. You may have noticed that the man was already rich. Probably rating eight, nine, or even ten talents in the gift-from-God category. Yet, he disappointed God to the point that our Creator called him home prematurely. Now, let's examine where our brother went wrong. It appears he was on the right road by tilling the ground so that it produced a great harvest.

I believe Christ is showing us in this passage that there was nothing wrong with the brother producing a great harvest, just as there is absolutely nothing wrong with us making money, producing in our lives, and even obtaining wealth. Where I believe the rich man went wrong was not in his great harvest but in what he did *with* the crop.

He reasoned with himself and concluded: "I will tear down *my barns* and build *bigger ones*, and there I will store all *my grain and my goods*. And, I'll say to *myself, 'You* have plenty of good things *laid up* for many years. *Take life easy, eat, drink, and be merry.'*"

First of all, he took full credit for his gains. Secondly, it did not appear, in the parable that Christ shared, that he tithed to the LORD or made any gesture of thanksgiving. Thirdly, he already had plenty of storage space that apparently was full, but as greed would have it, it was not enough. For some of us, it will never be enough.

Have you ever thought, beloved, what would be enough for you? I often ponder over that question when I read of the millions and billions that some people accumulate and appear to still want more.

As a matter of fact, a great number of news reporting is on the super-rich clawing and fighting to obtain more riches at the expense of the poor and the have-nots, whether it is through paying a disproportionately lower tax, corporate and tax loopholes, overseas tax-free savings accounts, and on, and on, and on.

This brings me to a political point of argument that I have taken a position on for years. Some argue that higher taxes on the wealthy will hurt the economy. They argue that fewer taxes on the rich will allow the rich to invest in the economy and create jobs. Please, let's be for real, if a rich person, who makes their money on the economy were to pay more taxes, they would still invest because that is how they make their money. The taxes they pay are irrelevant because they will still make their profits. No, they will not be able to keep as much, so, they will not be able to invest enough to make billions, just millions. Personally, I believe that is exactly what this parable is addressing. How much is enough?

Now, don't get me wrong, some rich people do very well with their blessings. We have some wealthy people who have proven to be great philanthropists and contributors to the advancement of society, as well as relieving the suffering of the poor.

That's not what this passage is about, nor am I advocating that there is something wrong with being wealthy. Christ was pointing out greed. He was exposing the heart and intent of this certain rich person choosing to keep it all to himself and claiming all was his when, in fact, "All things come of thee, O LORD," and we should further say: "And of thine own, have we given thee" by rendering our tithes (one tenth of our first fruit) and offering to God. All belongs to God.

What we have or have obtained is only a gift from God for which we are to be good stewards.

Have you ever wondered why Christ used that parable in responding to the man who asked him to convince his brother to share the inheritance with him? Well, I believe he was showing another side of greed. In the Hebrew custom, the elder son is in line for the family estate. What the elder son does with the estate is at his discretion. I found this hard to comprehend, but that is the custom. We know through our Biblical reading there were a few exceptions: Ishmael (Genesis 17:15–22) with Abraham's estate; Esau (Genesis 25:29–34) missed his inheritance due to his lack of discipline; and, of course, Manasseh (Genesis 48:8–20). But, I am still trying to understand why the custom.

I believe, however, that Christ was trying to show that greed and covetousness sometimes work hand in hand. After all, what was the motivation for the brother to ask Christ to do such a thing? Greed and covetousness. Covetousness is when you claim or desire something that is not yours. You do not have to take or possess the item to be guilty of covetousness. You should not even desire it. The inheritance was not his, nor, by custom, should he have asked for it. There is a saying: "Mother

121

may have, Father may have, but God blessed the Child that got his own." As unfair as the custom appeared to be, the LORD does not want us to desire something that is not ours. This is to keep us from exercising other means of the devil, like stealing or, one of the most common causes for world wars, wanting to enlarge our territory without merit.

A brother came into the pastor's office to request prayer from the good reverend. He informed his pastor that he was being considered for a promotion that would double his salary from $500 per week to $1,000 per week—a huge and life-changing advancement for him. He vowed that if he got the job, he would tithe, which was something that could not be done before because of his student loan and other financial obligations. The pastor obliged and offered a wonderful uplifting and soul-comforting prayer for the Christian gentleman. Sure enough, the brother got the job, and as promised, he started tithing at $75 per week; after all, his take home pay after taxes was $750.

A year later, the brother came into the pastor's office and again asked for prayer because another great opportunity presented itself. This time, his pay would be increased to approximately $2,000 per week.

Well, the pastor prayed, and wouldn't you know it, the brother got the job paying $2,000 per week. Life was good, so good that the gentleman was offered an executive position with all the perks, bonuses, and a salary of more than $5,000 per week. But, the pastor noticed no increase in the brother's giving and that the brother was still rendering $150 per week, which was reflective of his net pay at his $2,000-per-week position. So, the good reverend called the brother into his office and inquired as to why since his offerings were not as he had vowed. The brother acknowledged, "No Pastor, I am still paying the $150-per-week offering because I just purchased a new house, and my children are in private schools. Of course, I could not keep driving that common car, as I have an image to uphold with my executive position."

"Wow!" responded the pastor. "Sounds like your life is quite demanding now and you are juggling a lot. But, I have also noticed that besides having not increased your tithes, your service to the church ministries has decreased."

"Now, Pastor," he abruptly responded, "all you think about is money. I am paying a good share. As a matter of fact, I am probably the highest giver in the church. I know you are OK because I heard you got a new Chevy. Besides, $500 per week is an awful lot to give to this church. Oh, did I mention that I will not be at church every Sunday as before because I now can hold membership at the country club where the golf tournament is held? And that is where I meet with the board members. You don't understand, I have a lot on my plate, I don't know how I'm going to manage, so pray for me."

"I will," said the pastor, "as a matter of fact, let's do that now?" The brother agreed. This was the pastor's prayer:

Dear Lord, it's us again, praying for your mercy and grace. My brother here is finding it so difficult managing the life that you blessed him with, so LORD, maybe you should return him to his $2,000-per-week job so he can render unto you what he did, and not have so much on his plate.

The brother started to tithe $500 per week and work weekly in his church.

Like the rich fool in the Luke passage, the Church brother lost focus on what he should do with his gift. God wants us successful and to enjoy life, but we are not to be enslaved by our accomplishments and forget about our obligation to our Creator.

We don't have to give it all, just 10 percent of our time, talent, and earthly substance, and the rest is ours. Now, as in the brother's case, he could have used his resources to support the church's outreach, missionaries, and the many other enterprises of the church. That is what Christ said in Luke 12:31:

But seek [God's] kingdom, and these things will be given to you as well.

God does not want to deny us, unless it is for growth or something out of God's will for us. I believe we were created to enjoy God's creation and all of God's blessings that come with it. But Christ went further in Luke 12 in the thirty-fourth verse:

For where your treasure is, there your heart will be also.

Here Christ was clearly showing that it was not money, accomplishments, wealth, or possessions but the heart. What is your intent, purpose, and attitude in gaining riches? In the forty-eighth verse of the same chapter, Jesus hits us with another bombshell:

But the one who does not know and does things deserving punishment will be beaten with few blows. From everyone who has been given much, much will be demanded; and from the one who has been entrusted with much, much more will be asked.

Now, for those who have much, I believe there is another scripture that bears study and understanding. My dear mother shared it with me when she thought I was spending too much of my time skipping church to work overtime or be at a second job:

What profits a man to gain the world and forfeit his soul?

Mark 8:36

Although this is a true statement, it has been interpreted in such a way that common Christians may not have a clear understanding of what it actually means.

As a matter of fact, I have heard clergy use this scripture in an attempt to contradict having aspirations for wealth or financial success (whatever that means). I believe some clergy try to emphasize that one needs to see God's will in our lives and not focus on money alone as our main objective; they have the tendency to attach and play down wealth, unconsciously, of course. They sometimes talk against the capitalist system that we live in and downplay the free market that has made our country great. Although there are some flukes in our system, like the great meltdown of Wall Street we experienced in 2008, most flukes are sparked by humans driven by greed rather than a flaw in the economic or capitalist system. I believe in our democratic capitalistic system of government, although I believe we can do a better job in handling others who are less fortunate. Some teach that God does not care how financially successful we are. *Yes, God does*, because stewardship is a requirement of God, and what we do with what we have does matter. If we are good stewards, it will lead to financial gain. Now, what we need to understand is that whatever we gain is Jehovah's, and we should use it to God's glory.

The rich man in Luke 12 tried to gain the world but instead lost his soul and was called home. My mother feared that I would be caught up in greed and forget my obligation to Jehovah. It was her belief, and now mine, that all that I have belongs to God, and Jehovah wants me to have it, but God also requires my dedication, worship, and praise in my daily living.

My mother was not concerned about my tithing; she was concerned with my stewardship because she felt it was not about the money I gave but the blessings I shared in serving as well as giving.

Skipping church was a sign to her of me not serving God in addition to me not giving because I was not there, and like most people who skip church, I usually skipped tithing as well. Stewardship is more than giving; it is a process or way of life in which we surrender our time, talent, and earthly substance to God. It is also an attitude and posture of life, and she was afraid that I would have lost my grip.

Although I was slightly offended and a little insulted, that was Mother talking, and I would not dare respond as I felt. Later in life, I understood what she was trying to convey to me. All that I have belongs to Almighty Everlasting God, the Creator and sustainer of life, and all blessings come from HIM. What I do with my life is for God's glory and praise. No, God is not expecting me to give it all to the poor and live as a monk, but God does require me to have a spirit of stewardship, benevolence, and praise.

I often heard complaints about how famous and wealthy people are not doing enough to help the poor and disenfranchised. Well, are we sure about that? I'm not CNN or the IRS where I can search the records, but I sometimes hear a lot of philanthropic gestures from Bill Gates, Warren Buffet, Oprah Winfrey, and others who have been very

active in giving. But, those same critics may not even tithe. That means they did not learn from the Matthew parable.

You see, in that parable, it was not the rich that got into trouble with the LORD, it was the one who appeared to have received the least. Why? Because he buried his blessings and made excuses as to why he could not produce. Because of that, I believe God looks at the intent, attitude, and actions of our heart. I have heard complaints about the rich from persons who don't even give a tenth to the LORD, not to mention going further and helping others who are not as blessed as they are. Some of those folks are right in our churches, going to the Food Bank or Missionary Outreach Ministries, who find it so annoying to receive a request from someone in need, even when it is not their money but the church's because those same individuals have not tithed or given much of their earthly substance to the LORD. Why? Because they have the same heart as the servant with one talent; a lack of dedication, and stewardship. Some of them will tell you that they are serving in the Food Bank or Missionary Outreach as an exchange because they feel they cannot tithe. That may be the case for some, but if you watch others, observe how they operate the Benevolent Ministries. You may find that servant with that same one-talent servant is still with us, alive and functioning, just as unproductive as in Matthew 25, right under our nose.

I remember serving as an assistant pastor at my home church, where I convinced my pastor and congregation to host a Homeless Week. It was a program that the homeless shelter proposed to churches during the winter months when the shelters became full and had to turn people away. Our church was large and with a comfortable amount of rooms to accommodate the program.

We would welcome our guests in the evening with dinner, allow them to sleep inside the church complex at night, and as they woke in the morning, we would feed them breakfast and give them a bag lunch as they left that morning, only to see them come back that evening to start the process again. We would do this for seven days and then transfer them to the next church. This was a great program because, for the most part, churches are empty during the week, with very little activity, but the heat is still on, with steam coming out of the chimney, showing the vast waste of energy while people were out in the cold freezing to death. It was a worthwhile project with immediate gratification to those who served.

One day, we had a guest (we tried to train our volunteers to treat them as our special guests) who was quite large in stature. He stood about six feet, three inches tall and weighed around 200 to 250 pounds. As he came through the dinner line, the server placed a scoop of mashed potatoes from one of those ice cream scoopers on his plate. In a very humble and kind voice, the gentleman asked if he could have another scoop. To everyone's surprise, the server very sharply replied, "No, if you want more food, get a job!"

Oh my God, not good; not good at all.

If anyone says, "I love God," yet hates his brother, he is a liar. For anyone who does not love his brother, whom he has seen, cannot love God, whom he has not seen. And he has given us this command: Whoever loves God must also love his brother.

1 John 4:20–21

That one-talent servant had shown up again. It was not the money or potatoes, but the server took ownership of the food and refused to respond to a mere request from someone who may not have been as blessed and fortunate as they were.

Yet, the server used that opportunity (unconsciously, I believe) to pour salt on a wounded heart. A poor and uncaring heart or attitude can be just as nonproductive as burying your talent.

No matter how little you think you may have, you are still in a position to produce, to give, and to contribute, just as Warren Buffet, Bill Gates, Oprah Winfrey, President Barack Obama, and the woman who gave the Widow's Mite. Maybe you are not able to contribute at their level or at the rate that they give, but you are a child of the most High God and, therefore, gifted with a blessing for someone.

Just like the Rich Fool, just like the brother in the church, it was not what they had, rather it was their intent, their desire—it was where their heart was.

Therefore, as we have opportunity, let us do good to all people, especially to those who belong to the family of believers.

Galatians 6:10

I had a conversation with a friend of mine. As a matter of fact, she is a colleague of mine that helped me in my development as an educator. Her brother became very ill, and his wife willingly devoted all her time taking care of him. A member of their church came over to ask if they could do anything to help. You see, they were members of a church that taught its congregation to live with Galatians 6:10 in mind. The wife was very reluctant and fearful that if she was to accept she may not be viewed as a good wife. She voiced to my colleague, a very wise woman of God, that the person did not have the skills to do what really needed to be done anyway, that they would only hire someone to do the task for them.

To the wife's surprise, my colleague reminded her that it was that person's duty and that she may have stopped a blessing, not only for herself but for the person seeking to help, because that is what God-fearing believers do, particularly in their respective church membership.

The wife repeated to my colleague that the person probably could not have performed the task that needed to be done, likely hiring someone else to do it instead. My wise colleague reiterated that it did not matter what little skills the person had, that that person was willing to do anything to help: wash dishes, sweep the floor, and, yes, even hire someone with the skills to do whatever needed to be done.

You see, beloved, it is not the volume, complexity, quality, or impact of your gift or talent, it is the intent, spirit, purpose, and usage of your gift and how it can be a blessing for others.

When the Son of Man comes in his glory, and all the angels with him, he will sit on his throne in heavenly glory. All the nations will be gathered before him, and he will separate the people one from another as a shepherd separates the sheep from the goats. He will put the sheep on his right and the goats on his left. Then the King will say to those on his right, "Come, you who are blessed by my Father, take your inheritance, the kingdom prepared for you since the creation of the world. For I was hungry and you gave me something to eat, I was thirsty and you gave me something to drink, I was a stranger and you invited me in, I needed clothes and you clothed me, I was sick and you looked after me, I was in prison and you came to visit me." Then the righteous will answer him, "Lord, when did we see you hungry and feed you, or thirsty and give you something to drink? When did we see you a stranger and invite you in, or needing clothes and clothe you? When did we see you sick or in prison and go to visit you?" The King will reply, "I tell you the truth, whatever you did for the one of the least of these brothers of mine, you did for me."

Matthew 25:31–40

Remember the warning at the end of the Matthew passage of the talents.

Please do something with your heavenly given gift. Don't start making excuses about your life and why you didn't do anything with it. No matter how little you think you may have or what your circumstances may appear to be, the creator has placed you on this earth for a reason, especially if you were born in America, the land of the free, where time after time we read how people were born in poverty and all kinds of helpless surroundings and circumstances, yet they achieved. It is really up to you. Take that one talent, my brother and sister, use it; it is really up to you.

I remember working with a young man who always complained and made excuses as to why he did not achieve. Like the servant in the Matthew scripture, he blamed the owners of the company, management, and the shareholders that were making money on his back through his hard work (even though he did not come to work that often because he had been disciplined for absenteeism and tardiness). He felt he was not being properly compensated. I remember having a conversation with a coworker one day when I said to him; maybe he was right but asked if he considered investing in the company's 401-k plan.

"Of course not," he replied.

"I thought you said they were making money on your back, on your hard work?" I responded.

"Yes, I did say that," he replied.

Then, I explained, "Why not turn the tables and start making money on your own back.

"If you can't own the company, you can at least buy part of it and get some of the money that they are making on your hard labor." Of course, the brother didn't see my point.

But, whatever the case may be, God will call us home one day, and we all will have to account for our journey and mission. God will reconcile with us as to what we have done with our individual talent, gift, blessings, and earthly life. For Jehovah has given each and every one a gift, and with that gift or talent a charge to do his will or carry out our given mission, with some pretty good benefits through his grace, love, and mercy.

The creator did not design our lives for us to complain although some of us have had some pretty disappointing moments. I do not believe that was In God's plan for humankind. God, like the mother SHE is, supplied us with all we need for a successful life and sent us on our way, eager to see what we would do with our mission during our earthly journey. Now, don't get me wrong, God can, at times, intervene and get directly involved in the affairs of humanity. However, Elohim usually leaves it up to us. That's why God created us in HIS image.

Therefore, our job or "Life Challenge" is to take what God has given us and use it to the best of our ability and faith to produce a wonderful life that we can face God with after our life on earth is done and hear the words that we all would love to hear:

"Well done, my good and faithful servant."

.

CHAPTER EIGHT

ATTITUDE

Your Attitude Determines Your Altitude

Therefore, I urge you, brothers, in view of God's mercy, to offer your bodies as living sacrifices, holy and pleasing to God—this is your spiritual act of worship. Do not conform any longer to the pattern of this world, but be transformed by the renewing of your mind. Then you will be able to test and approve what God's will is—his good, pleasing, and perfect will.

Romans 12:1–2

That means, beloved, you need to first renew your mind. You can't think the way the world thinks and succeed. Success is not derived by using common sense. Why, because common sense is reasoning that a common or average person uses in their decision-making process. Well, beloved, what if I told you that God has given us guidelines on making decisions and that there is nothing *common* about it. To be common is to be average, the norm, or do what the majority of the people would do. That is not how Christians or any God-fearing person makes their decisions. Many achievers in history were labeled different, weird, and, in some cases, freaks. Now, of course, you don't want to be labeled as any of these, although Peter did say that we were a peculiar people, in other words, we are different. One of the ways we are different is that we seek first the kingdom of God in our lives. We first must strive to do God's will in our lives. Secondly, as Romans 12 indicates, we have to declare and render ourselves a living sacrifice to God by living to glorify Elohim in our lives.

The letter to the Romans tells us that whatever gift we have; we must use it to glorify God in our lives. Once we know who we are, what we have, and to whom we belong, we are on our way to success. So, don't stop, don't quit, for you are special, peculiar, and different because God made you that way. Now, you need to develop the attitude of a winner.

In an online advertisement of Lumiday.com, they published a very interesting piece of literature I thought would fit very well here. "A poor mood wears and tears on your body, leaving you feeling tired, drained, and empty inside. It's incredibly tough to be successful when your mind and body are working against you or just not up to par. Unhappiness can damage your relationship, hurt your family and friends, and make every day a struggle." When I read that, I thought of a negative or defeatist attitude that a person develops when giving up. It not only pulls you down, it can affect everybody around you, and particularly the ones you love. Have you ever experienced or lived with someone with a defeatist's attitude? It is extremely difficult to be enthused yourself because they seem to pull you down with them. When you feel defeated, your health is even affected because everything appears to give in to a failure mode.

His master replied, "You wicked, lazy servant! So you knew that I harvest where I have not sown and gather where I have not scattered seed? Well then, you should have put my money on deposit with the bankers, so that when I returned I would have received it back with interest. Take the talent from him and give it to the one who has the ten talents."

Matthew 25: 26–28

I am very careful not to call it laziness, so I will say defeatist or having a negative attitude. Somehow, some way, Satan convinced the servant to bury his talent, the gift God gave him, or just sit on it and not use the gift of God. Please, beloved, don't let that happen to you, discover your God-given gift—perfect it, use it, produce with it, and be blessed by it.

God does not want defeat in us, my friend. That is the spirit of the devil. Cast it out of your life; you are a child of a King, the creator of heaven and earth, the maker and master of all good things. God made you in HER own image to be an achiever, a winner, a custodian of the earth, an inventor, earthly creator, procreator, ambassador of Yahweh, and a disciple of Christ. Therefore, negative thoughts should never be allowed in our thinking.

Like a city whose walls are broken down is a man who lacks self-control.

Proverbs 25:28

Take control of your life: be that winner, let the light shine in your heart, mind, and soul so that God can continue to use and bless you and others through *your* marvelous works. Don't give in to Satan, Just Don't Quit.

During my career in the corporate world, I had the opportunity to enter into a management-development program. This was a program that was offered to college graduates who had aspirations of becoming corporate managers (so I thought). I learned a lot about attitudes and positive thinking. We were taught that, when given a task that seemed out of the box or revolutionary, we should never respond to the leader with the words "we can't do that" or "it cannot be done," rather we were to first respond by asking ourselves, "How can we accomplish this?" or "What are the possibilities?" Believe it or not, it worked.

When we discovered a problem, we were not allowed to go into the boss's office just to inform them of the problem we were facing; rather, we presented the *challenge* with at least three suggestions on how to meet that challenge.

We were also taught that no team can survive with a negative-thinking member. If we had anyone on the team who lacked confidence in the achievement of the team, that person had to be dealt with quickly, otherwise they would become a cancer for the team. That's when I began to learn the treacherous characteristic of the corporate world, for if that person could not be turned around to a positive state in a very short period of time, they would be eliminated.

Thank God that Jehovah does not work that way with us. SHE is merciful and forgiving and has made provisions for our shortcomings by sending us a Savior, a Comforter, to fill the void in our character.

That corporate method created a frame of mind that all problems were solvable. Like training a little child to eat, we feed them at first. We literally place the food in the child's mouth from the time we wean them from the bottle until we think it is time for them to eat on their own. For some of us, like me, our mothers had to just place the spoon on the table as we cried for them to feed us. After a while of leaving us to cry and whine, we finally got up enough courage, or hunger, to pick up the utensil and start the process of feeding ourselves.

No, it was not easy or very neat, but, eventually, we got the hang of it. The corporate world taught me to try, push myself beyond my comfort zone, and dare to venture, for if I didn't, I would be eliminated.

Do you remember the story of the "Survival of the Lepers?"

Now there were four men with Leprosy at the entrance of the city gate. They said to each other, "Why stay here until we die? If we say, 'We'll go into the city'—the famine is there, and we will die. And if we stay here we will die. So let's go over to the camp of the Arameans and surrender. If they spare us, we live; if they kill us, then we die." At dusk they got up and went to the camp of the Arameans. When they reached the edge of the camp, not a man was there, for the Lord had caused the Arameans to hear the sound of chariots and horses and a great army, so that they said to one another, "Look, the king of Israel has hired the Hittite and Egyptian kings to attack us!" So they got up and fled in the dusk and abandoned their tents and their horses and donkeys. They

*left the camp as it was and ran for their lives. The men who had lep-
rosy reached the edge of the camp and entered one of the tents. They
ate and drank, and carried away silver, gold, and clothes and went off
and hid them. They returned and entered another tent and took some
things from it and hid them also.*

2 Kings 7:3–8

Those poor men were in what appeared to be a lose-lose situation, but because of their positive thinking, although it seemed mighty
bleak, they dared to try. Life is like that, my friend. You may find yourself in a very hopeless situation, a helpless state, yet with a positive
attitude, with unwavering faith, you can overcome.

I can do everything through him who gives me strength.

Philippians 4:13

**Let the LORD be exalted, who delights in the
well-being of his servant.**

Psalm 35:27

Please understand, beloved, God wants you successful, but HE will
not throw it down from the sky like the children of Israel in the wilderness. SHE has designed life to be pursued by HER creation, which is
you. God has given you the tools and the means of getting it all, but we
need to connect on to that vine we talked about. We need to renew our
minds and not think like the world; we need to think, walk, live, and be
different in order to succeed.

Sometimes, God places us in position to prosper, although we may
not see it at the time. Esther had such an experience. You know the

135

story, she found herself queen at a time when Haman appeared to have had the upper hand in eliminating the Jews.

But Mordecai petitioned Esther to approach the king on behalf of her people. Initially she refused, saying:

All the king's officials and the people of the royal provinces know that for any man or woman who approaches the king in the inner court without being summoned the king has but one law; that he be put to death. The only exception to this is for the king to extend the gold scepter to him and spare his life.

Esther 4:11

But, Mordecai responded with a challenge and warning:

He sent back this answer: "Do not think that because you are in the king's house you alone of all the Jews will escape. For if you remain silent at this time, relief and deliverance for the Jews will arise from another place, but you and your father's family will perish. And who knows but that you have come to royal position for such a time as this?"

Esther 4:13–14

Although God was not mentioned in this passage of scripture, we know that God placed Esther In that position to do what appeared to be the impossible, and after the praying and fasting and believing, she took on a positive attitude and was successful in saving her people.

Now, beloved, I have to be very truthful with you: that was giving God the glory. But, we would not notice or believe it if the triumph was over any other situation but one that appears to be all but impossible. It is very difficult for man to give God the credit for things within his reach. When man triumphs out of very difficult and sometimes impossible situations, we know that God is in control. We must believe, conceive, trust, and have that positive attitude that only comes from our faith.

Bishop John Richard Bryant, senior bishop of the African Methodist Episcopal Church, wrote an article in *The Anvil* that was entitled, "A New Attitude." In that article, he testified how God used him in his early ministry while he was assigned to a church in Cambridge, Massachusetts. He described his church as an older congregation that, for all practical purposes, was on their way out. Most of the people there were old and pretty set in their ways. Like the lepers, they were at the brink of spiritual hopelessness. But, God gave this brilliant servant a vision to have a revival, not at the run-down church where they were but on the grounds of the Massachusetts Institute of Technology's (MIT) auditorium. Wow! Like Esther, this was never done before and was sort of forbidden. After all, how would you even approach this Ivy League institution of higher learning with such a religious concept?

Well, through prayer, fasting, and faith in positive thinking, he not only convinced his congregation, he also convinced MIT. Not only was the worship service a success, his membership exploded.

We can talk about a number of God's servants who dared to think and act beyond common thought or common reasoning and by faith and positive attitude that changed not only their circumstances but those of the world as well:

Martin Luther
Bishop Richard Allen
Evangelist Billy Graham
The Reverend Dr. Martin Luther King Jr.
The Reverend Benny Hen

But, I don't want you to think we are only talking about ministers; God has blessed us all with various gifts and talents to do HER will, and with faith and a positive attitude.

Society has benefited from the great accomplishments of:

The Wright Brothers
Albert Einstein
Harriet Tubman
George Washington
George Washington Carver
Drs. Charles Drew and Ben Carson

God has made each and every one of us special with unique gifts and graces, but not for us to brag, boast, and certainly not to bury. But we do need to adopt that positive attitude, that faith that allows us to think outside of the box, to stretch beyond our comfort zone and reach where the common populous may have doubt and even fear. We are to be fearless and courageous with faith that God has given us all that we need to succeed by trusting and believing—and putting that belief into action within faith itself.

But you are a chosen people, a royal priesthood, a holy nation, a people belonging to God, that you may declare the praises of HIM who called you out of the darkness into HIS wonderful light.

I Peter 2:9

This does not make you special to the point of flaunting; rather, it makes you special to the point of being an ambassador for peace, love, joy, and, most of all, salvation for others. Because of your peculiarity, or your spiritual status, you may be the only Christian that someone may see; and because of that, you may be the only one who can offer them salvation and bring them to Christ. What an awesome privilege; what an awesome opportunity.

Yes, all of that is in you, my friend:

I tell you the truth, anyone who has faith in me will do what I have been doing. He will do even greater things than these, because I am going to the Father. And I will do whatever you ask in my name, so that the Son may bring glory to the Father. You may ask me for anything in my name, and I will do it.

John 14:12–14

Jesus also said:

You are the salt of the earth. But if the salt loses its saltiness, how can it be made salty again? It is no longer good for anything, except to be thrown out and trampled by men.

You are the light of the world. A city on a hill cannot be hidden. Neither do people light a lamp and put it under a bowl. Instead they put it on its stand, and it gives light to everyone in the house. In the same way, let your light shine before men, that they may see your good deeds and praise your Father in heaven.

Matthew 5:13–16

God has made you the light of this world—the hope of humanity. Therefore, you have something to share that will be a blessing for others. Our passage reminds us that we cannot bury our blessings, we must let them shine. In other words, "Let the life you live, speak for you." You are the hope for this world; you are the representative of God's creation. So, you can't just let the gifts in you stay dormant, you have to release them so that it will be a blessing for you and others.

You may ask, "But what is my blessing, what did God give me that's so special? Because I don't see it." Well, that is also where church membership, fellowship, and worship come in. Although church cannot save you, church is established to teach us how to pray, fast, meditate, discover, and develop our spiritual gifts. You may not see your special blessing right away, but, trust me, my friend, it is there. One of the challenges of life is to find ourselves. What we are about and what we are capable of doing to contribute to the betterment of our society and world. This is where your pastor(s), teacher(s), and other spiritual leader(s) can help.

139

It was he who gave some to be apostles, some to be prophets, some to be evangelists, and some to be pastors and teachers, to prepare God's people for works of service, so that the body of Christ may be built up until we all reach unity in the faith and in the knowledge of the Son of God and become mature, attaining to the whole measure of the fullness of Christ. Then we no longer be infants, tossed back and forth by the waves, and blown here and there by every wind of teaching and by the cunning and craftiness of men in their deceitful scheming.

Ephesians 4:11–14

It is not uncommon to be unaware of your spiritual gifts and talents, but it is our duty to find it and use it to further the kingdom.

I remember having a conversation with an individual who was disturbed about things that they saw and which needed to be changed. They used that situation to question the existence of God. After all, why would God allow so many bad things to happen? I took them the story about an old lady who lived alone. She only received social security, and it was very hard to make ends meet. It was the middle of the month after spending her last dollar on medication, and she realized her food would not last until the beginning of the next month when she would receive her next Social Security check. She started to pray and ask God for help. On this particular day, two young and devilish (as the old folks would call them) boys overheard her prayer out of an open window. "Let's play a trick on her," one said to the other. So, they put their monies together and went to the grocery store. They bought some eggs, milk, and, for the most part, did a pretty good job of shopping for long-lasting edibles.

They returned to the home of the elderly woman, placed the grocery bag in front of her door, rang the doorbell, and hid behind the bushes. As the old lady opened the door to discover the food, she began shouting—praising and thanking God.

"Oh, thank you, Lord. You are so good to me, praise your holy name."

140

The young men jumped from the bushes, laughing and joking with the lady: "Silly lady, God didn't send that food, we bought it from store." She replied, "Oh yeah, God sent the food all right. He may have used a couple of demons to deliver it, but He sent it all right!"

I then explained to them that God uses humanity to help humanity. I believe it is one of the world's problems. Do you know we literally throw away enough food in America to feed the rest of the world? Yet, for economic reasons (not the system but the thinking), we will even pay farmers *not* to grow in some instances. I believe God is challenging us to do something about poverty and starvation, but we are failing the test—miserably.

Being a positive thinker with a productive attitude sometimes means you have to be very picky about who you befriend. My brother Marshall, who very seldom goes to church but seems to quote scripture more than anyone I know, illustrates and teaches in parables or sayings that I have later found in scripture. He is a very wise man in counseling. The type of person you would never expect, but one who is full of knowledge. He sort of adopted the role of mentor to me when our father died. Like my Drill Sergeant Mom, I felt that my big brother was a little hard on me at times, but I see him now as a gift from God.

He would say, "Never hang around a person that can't teach you anything. Your mind won't grow that way."

Or he would say, "Look, man, you can't soar like an eagle flying with turkeys."

He had another one, if I can remember: "If birds of a feather flock together, you better watch who you fly with, for association will bring participation."

Now that was heavy to me. But my favorite of his sayings was, "You got to be different to be better, and in this world, you got to be better to succeed."

I kept those thoughts with me, for all through life they became useful. I realized what he was saying is your friends and associates can influence your thinking, performance, and, eventually, your outcome. If you surround yourself with negative thinkers and doomsayers, it will affect you. Your surroundings create a force of positive or negative influence on you, and no matter how strong you think you are; your environment can affect your output. I don't think he meant to be arrogant for thinking of oneself as better than anyone else but to expect more of yourself.

I never was much on sports because of our economic conditions at home. I started working at age twelve and never had the opportunity to learn, practice, or perfect a sport. So, my athletic abilities left a lot (a whole lot) to be desired. But as I reflect on the days I did engage in sports, I seemed to perform better when playing with or against good players. Sometimes it takes us facing or working with those whom we can learn from to better ourselves.

Wilt Chamberlain, Larry Bird, and even Michael Jordan played their better games when they were surrounded by good players, whether on an opposite team or a team member.

I believe the same principle holds when it comes to living. Having a positive attitude of faith is also making sure that as many people, places, times, or circumstances you face are just as positive or even uplifting and encouraging. This is another strong argument for church membership. Now, I agree, not everyone in church is positive, but it is designed to be a positive force for all believers. Just as I have indicated before, every Sunday, I have my congregation chant, "Blessed, highly favored, and in a position to be a blessing!"

As we indicated before, we are all here for a purpose, a task, and a duty, but we won't be able to achieve our earthly goal without first knowing what it is, knowing our gifts and talents, and exercising that faith and positive attitude.

So, be that beacon of light for others to see, and be that guiding light for others to follow. You cannot do that with a defeatist attitude; you must develop that:

Attitude of a Winner.

CHAPTER NINE

NURTURE

Continue to Grow and Glow in Christ

In Chapter Three, we learned that we are required to develop a healthy lifestyle in order to take care of this temple that God has put in our trust for our earthly journey. Well, there is another body to which we are entrusted, and that is our spiritual body or spiritual being.

Merriam-Webster defines nurture as, "The caring for and encouraging the growth of someone or something. It is to be involved in the orchestration of bringing up; nourish; nursing, rearing; breeding or feeding of someone of something." To nurture is to cultivate, mold, shape, and develop someone or something. We nurture our children, students, and, in the case of preachers, teachers, and pastors, we nurture our flock or congregation and other believers. But in order to nurture someone or something else, we have to obtain the capability to nurture. That means, we too have to be nurtured to the point of being able to nurture others.

When we are aboard a commercial airliner, the first thing the flight attendant does is go over the safety regulations of flying. If you are like me, you get tired of hearing it every time you board a plane. But, we know that it is necessary for our safety. You probably know what the flight attendant will say word for word if you are a frequent flyer.

"If by chance we have a sudden loss of air pressure, the air bags will automatically drop. Place the oxygen mask over your nose and mouth, and slightly pull the elastic band to tighten the air bag. If you have a child with you, place the air bag on yourself first, then place the air bag on the child."

Our spiritual journey is like that flight-safety demonstration: we have to first equip ourselves before we can help anyone else. There was a joke about one of our previous presidents, who was asked why he did not come to the defense of one of his aides who got into political hot water and was about to face criminal charges. His response was, "How can you save a man from drowning when your own ship is sinking?" You must first nurture yourself, strengthen yourself, and prepare yourself before you can help others.

Before a mother can properly nurse her child, she needs to nurture herself, for what is in her will eventually be in that baby. If she smokes, drinks, and takes substances of a harmful nature, there is a good chance that it will affect the baby that she is trying to nurture. The same goes for our spiritual nurturing; we must have good, solid spiritual nutrition in order to be in the position to nurture others.

In Chapter Six, when we talked about integrity, I shared different versions of the Bible and argued that they will differ in their reading. Well, this is one reference that differs so much I will deviate from my regular NIV reading to KJV:

Study to show thyself approved unto God, a workman that needeth not to be ashamed, rightly dividing the word of truth. But shun profane and vain babblings for they will increase unto more ungodliness.

2 Timothy 2:15–16 (KJV)

Spiritual nurturing begins with studying the WORD of God. Part of claiming your inheritance is knowing of what your heritage consists. How would you know someone left you with an inheritance if you did not even associate yourself with the benefactor or know that you were even considered as an heir, especially if you were not born into the family? But, what if I told you that you can be an heir without being born into a particular family as long as you are *Born Again* into a specific family?

144

To be born again into that family of rich heritage, you need to follow the instruction maps our Lord and Savior left for us in Romans 10:9:

That if you confess with your mouth, "Jesus is Lord," and believe in your heart that God raised him from the dead, you will be saved.

STUDY

The more you study the WORD, the more reference you have in your decision-making process. It strengthens your intellect and allows you to grow in knowledge and understanding, and it exposes you to wisdom, which is the ability to apply God's word to our lives effectively and appropriately. Now, studying the WORD is more than reading the Bible; it's continuously subjecting yourself to content study of the what, when, where, how, and, most importantly, the why of the Biblical scriptures. Studying the WORD is a systematic process of exegetical analysis of the scripture that may require formal study classes, second-party assistance, and even aid from other sources, like commentaries, books, articles, and, please, don't forget your pastor. For clergy, another minister that you trust to correct you when they feel you are misinterpreting the WORD, are off track, or need to dig a little deeper.

The most impressive and assuring words I have gotten from my biblical colleagues was, "I don't know about that, let me do some research and call you back on that." All of this must accompany prayer, prayer, and more prayer.

MEDITATE

During your studies, you may often come across instructions and guides that may be a little difficult to digest. Not everything we read in the Bible is easy to adopt in our lives. This is not when we ignore or claim it's not applicable. This is the time for us to meditate on that lesson and keep asking ourselves why it is so difficult to make that adjustment in our lives. Through meditation, it allows our discerning spirit to manifest in us and open our spiritual eyes to the truth as to why this item is giving us a challenge.

It is also through meditation that we are re-connected to the Vine. When this happens, we get a second wind in our struggle and can actually be empowered to overcome that mental, emotional, and spiritual obstacle that may be hindering our growth. This too is always preceded by prayer, prayer, and more prayer.

Meditation is not just closing our eyes and taking deep breaths and waiting to hear from the LORD. Although it's a start, your body, mind, and spirit must be clear of all spiritual debris. I find it difficult to meditate on a full or empty stomach. Your body must be relaxed, both internally as well as externally. So your body can't be craving for food. This is why fasting is so very important. Why? Because fasting puts the body under control.

If your body is full, then your flesh in satisfied (temporarily), but then the focus is on the flesh, and it is very difficult to get the full benefits of meditation when your body is busy digesting food and catering to the flesh. Your spirit needs to be free to connect to the VINE.

STRESS CONTROL

Although stress is dangerous and can be very harmful to our health and state of being, it is also a good indicator that we are on the right track. Stress is when there is a contrast in our life. There is something inside of us that has met some form of resistance. It does not always involve someone pressing our buttons; rather, it could be something blocking our growth. You may need to use the Mark 9:29 approach:

This kind can come out only by prayer.

But, I want to be clear and very careful here. All stress is not spiritual in nature, and even if it is, it's not all because we are in the growth process. Some of us are stressed out because our spirits are troubled over worldly things.

Therefore I tell you, do not worry about your life, what you will eat or drink; or about your body, what you will wear. Is not life more important than food, and the body more important than clothes? Look at the birds of the air; they do not sow or reap or store away in barns, and yet your heavenly Father feeds them. Are you not much more valuable than they? Who of you by worrying can add a single hour to his life?

And why do you worry about clothes? See how the lilies of the field grow. They do not labor or spin. I tell you that not even Solomon in all his splendor was dressed like one of these. If that is how God clothes the grass of the field, which is here today and tomorrow is thrown into the fire, will HE not much more clothe you, O you of little faith? So do not worry saying, "What shall we eat?" or "What shall we wear?" For the pagans run after all these things, and your heavenly Father knows that you need them. But seek first HIS kingdom and his righteousness, and all these things will be given to you as well. Therefore do not worry about tomorrow, for tomorrow will worry about itself. Each day has enough trouble of its own.

Matthew 6:25–34

Of course, this is a metaphor used by Christ to paint a picture of how nonproductive worrying is for us. Most of our stress comes from worrying about things that are not of God and have very little to do with the kingdom or our relationship to Elohim. We cannot grow in God or nurture our spiritual being by worrying about worldly things. Does God want us to go naked? No, that's not Christ's point. Is Jesus implying we should go hungry? On the contrary, but don't be concerned as the pagan is.

What does that mean? Well, have you heard people say, "They eat well" or "They look good in clothes?" The world uses these areas of our lives, not just as survival but as a sort of status symbol. It is not that you don't have food but that you don't have the right food—not just to feed your body, but also your ego. Same with the clothes. So many times we are concerned about how we can dress to impress.

So to control stress is to get a grip on what's important to you: the Joneses or The Kingdom. Are you concerned about the world, society, friends, neighbors, and others? If so, you will more than likely always have stress. But, if you put your focus on the kingdom of heaven or the Will of God, you will have Stress control. How do I do that? Through prayer and more prayer.

PRAISE AND WORSHIP

There's a saying: "When praises go up, blessings come down." Sounds like a great cliché, doesn't it? Well, if you think about it, it holds a lot of truth. Praises are what we do to also connect with the Creator, and it is one of our many ways to offer thanksgiving and give honor and praise for what God has done for us. Remember the tactic you used when you wanted something from your parents. If you are male, you worked it best on Mom; and if you are female, it probably worked best on Dad. You cuddled next to them, maybe even stroked their hair and told them how much you loved them; you probably really poured it on when you told them what a fantastic parent they were and how proud and thankful you were just to be their child. They probably interrupted with the question, "OK, what do you want?" Even though they knew you were running a game on them, it probably worked more times than it failed. Why? Because of your *praise*.

God is our spiritual parent, and guess what? There are times that it works for us as well, so get your praise on.

Worship is man's way of acknowledging God for who and what SHE is: THE CREATOR, THE SUSTAINER, and THE DELIVERER of our lives. When we worship, we are lifting and praising the one, and only one, we depend on outside of ourselves. We are acknowledging that this is the very source of our help, strength, and hope.

We worship with praise and thanksgiving for the things that we have and the way of life that we enjoy. What greater source to refer to than the Book of Psalms?

I rejoiced with those who said to me, let us go to the house of the LORD. Our feet are standing in your gate, O Jerusalem. Jerusalem is built like a city that is closely compacted together.

Psalms 122:1–2

148

Or

Better is one day in your courts than a thousand elsewhere; I would rather be a doorkeeper in the house of my God than dwell in the tents of the wicked.

Psalm 84:10

Worship is essential to our connecting with the Holy One to renew our covenant with God and sustain our relationship that was afforded to us by our Lord and Savior, Jesus the Christ, which keeps us connected.

PRAYER AND FASTING

When you fast, do not look somber as the hypocrites do, for they disfigure their faces to show men they are fasting. I tell you the truth, they have received their reward in full. But when you fast, put oil on your head and wash your face, so that it will not be obvious to men that you are fasting, but only to your Father, who is unseen; and your Father, who sees what is done in secret, will reward you.

Matthew 6:16–18

Fasting is an exercise of self-denial, when we put our bodies under spiritual discipline. Many people are upset when I say this, but even Jesus had to put his body in check, under spiritual control, before he was able to start his ministry:

Then Jesus was led by the Spirit into the desert to be tempted by the devil. After fasting forty days and forty nights, he was hungry. The tempter came to him and said, "If you are the Son of God, tell these stones to become bread."

Jesus answered, "It is written: Man does not live on bread alone, but on every word that comes from the mouth of God." Then the devil took him to the holy city and had him stand on the highest point of the temple. "If you are the Son of God", he said, "throw yourself down. For it is written: 'He will command his angels concerning you, and they will lift you up in their hands, so that you will not strike your foot against a stone.'" Jesus answered him, "It is also written: Do not put the LORD your God to the test." Again, the devil took him to a very high mountain and showed him all the kingdoms of the world and their splendor. "All this I will give you," he said, "if you will bow down and worship me." Jesus said to him, "Away from me, Satan! For it is written: 'Worship the LORD your God, and serve him only.'" Then the devil left him, and angels came and attended him.

Matthew 4:1–11

You know the story. We have been reading about the Wilderness Experience for years. The scripture is often used around Lent season, reminding us that prayer and fasting is essential to our Christian growth, strength, and endurance. It doesn't matter whether we use the Matthew reference or the Luke; it still comes out the same. After his baptism, he went through a spiritual basic training, so to speak. His mind, body, and soul had to be conditioned to begin his ministry, and in order to do that, he needed to be prepared to endure that spiritual warfare that Satan prepared for him.

Allow me to mention that Jesus was tempted through his body by way of hunger, his mind by way of power, and his soul by way of his heart. We are also tempted via our body, mind and soul, although it may be in different ways and at different times. But, in order for us to be of service to God or experience all the blessing that God has in store for us, we must go through our Wilderness Experience, spiritual basic training, and we must overcome the tempter's test of our mind, body, and soul.

In Luke 4:13, the writer says something a little different. This was very interesting to me. He wrote:

When the devil had finished all this tempting, he left him until an opportune time.

I wonder, my friend, when was an opportune time?

Was it when he entered the temple and was challenged by the Sanhedrins and the Jewish Leaders?

(Mark 11:27–33; Luke 19:45–48, 20:1–8; John 2:12–19, 10:22–39)

Can you imagine the very person that baptized you may have questions about you?

(Matthew 11:1–6; Luke 7:18–23)

Or when he was called a demon?

(Matthew 12:22–37)

Was it an opportune time when his hometown took offense to him?

(Matthew 13:53–58; Mark 6:1–6; Luke 4:14–30)

When so many people were in need of food?

(Mark 6:30–44, 8:1–9; Luke 9:10–17; John 6:1–15)

What about the time when the disciples wanted to take matters into their hands?

(Luke 9:51–56; Luke 22:49–53; John 18:10–11)

Can you imagine not being able to mourn at the death of your own cousin?

(Matthew 14:6–14)

When the bravest of his disciples, displayed little faith?

(Matthew 14:25–33)

Can you imagine the doubting of his own family?

(John 7:2–5)

What about him being betrayed even with a kiss?

(Matthew 26:47–50; Mark 14:43–52; Luke 22:1–6, 47–48; John 6:60–71, 18:1–9)

Or the time when he was denied by one of his own?

(Mark 14:66–72; Luke 22:54–62; John 18:15–17)

Could it have been at the mock trial?

(Matthew 27:11–26; Luke 23:8–24; John 19:1–16)

Or was it the suffering that he endured on the cross?

(Matthew 27:27–56; Mark 15:16–39; Luke 23:32–43)

Well, beloved, it was all of the above and more. Now, the most important lesson of these scriptures is that as Satan tempted Jesus in many ways throughout his life and ministry, be assured that Satan will do the same to you. Please understand, just as the details of your wilderness experience or spiritual basic training will differ from Jesus's, so will Satan's temptation moments. This is why prayer and fasting is so very important for our Christian growth. You must be prayed up and faith solid; you need to know when, how, and where Satan will present himself, or herself, to you.

A good example was Joseph, Jacob's son. He knew he was being tested by Satan through Potiphar's wife. Because of his spiritual integrity, Joseph was able to weather the storm to follow as well (Genesis 39th Chapter).

But, in the case of Samson, he did not stay connected and had no clue that Delilah, the love of his life, was possessed by the evil one. Samson was spiritually blind, even when Delilah gave him warning sign after warning sign, because his mental capacity had also malfunctioned to the point he could not recognize Satan's attack (Judges 16th Chapter). Although he was gifted, blessed, and anointed to do God's will, without spiritual integrity, he buckled at the first sight of a pretty Philistine woman. Notice, by not being connected, it affected everything he did mentally and physically. As gifted as he was, it appeared that he never adhered to the rules of a Nazirite. I don't remember reading where Samson prayed or fasted before the LORD. Now, I may be wrong, but this leaves me with the impression that the strong, mighty, and powerful Samson lost his spiritual connection and, therefore, fizzled out.

We can say the same for David, a man after God's own heart. A mighty warrior and king of Israel who, to this day, is believed the greatest king who ever lived. Yet, he failed to walk in integrity because he was not connected. While his men were at war and he was left behind, he did not pray and fast for their victory; instead, he became weak enough for Satan to work on his flesh and present him some eye candy in the form of Uriah's wife (2 Samuel 11th Chapter). He was so out of it spiritually that Satan led him on a sinful roller coaster, and before he knew it, Nathan had to deliver some bad news that would plague his family for years to come. As a matter of fact, it plagued Israel so that they have yet to recover.

My friend, Satan is alive and well even today, and he is more than willing to put you and me to the test. This is his job, and he takes it seriously:

One day the angels came to present themselves before the LORD, and Satan also came with them. The LORD said to Satan, "Where have you come from?"

Satan answered the LORD, "From roaming through the earth and going back and forth in it."

Then the LORD said to Satan, "Have you considered my servant Job? There is no one on earth like him; he is blameless and upright, a man who fears God and shuns evil."

Job 1:6–8

My friend, this is proof Satan is doing his job and will continue to do his job to tempt you and me to do wrong. That is the mysterious contract of God that must come with free will. But, the good news is what preceded:

In the land of Uz there lived a man whose name was Job. This man was blameless and upright; he feared God and shunned evil. He had seven sons and three daughters, and he owned seven thousand sheep, three thousand camels, five hundred yoke of oxen, and five hundred donkeys, and had a large number of servants. He was the greatest man among all the people of the East.

His sons used to take turns holding feasts in their homes, and they would invite their three sisters to eat and drink with them. When a period of feasting had run its course, Job would send and have them purified. Early in the morning he would sacrifice a burnt offering for each of them, thinking, "Perhaps my children have sinned and cursed God in their hearts." This was Job's regular custom.

Job 1:1–5

Here we can clearly see that Job not only fasted and prayed, he offered sacrifices to the LORD on his children's behalf. One thing is for sure, beloved, Job was spiritually connected. And, because he was connected, he was able to go through the most painful and hideous suffering, second only to the crucifixion.

What I am saying to you, beloved, is that prayer and fasting is our spiritual defense against the devil and all of his trickery.

Meditation is for the mind.

Fasting is for the body.

Prayer is for the spirit.

REACTIVE ARTICLE
NURTURE

Indeed, our lives are fuller when we are connected to our Lord and Savior. The spiritual connection allows a direct line to the wisdom that—when we trust, have faith, and have made the decision required of us in Romans 10:8—provides us with the discernment needed to make wise decisions as we go about our daily lives. I cannot begin to count the number of times I have tapped into this connection to make decisions that affected my well-being, as well as those of others. You see, I start each day with a brief prayer of thanksgiving for the blessings of life, health, and the beauty of this world that God has provided. I follow it up with one request: please give me the wisdom that I need to make the right choices as I go about my day. I thank HIM in advance for this wonderful gift, and then, as always, ask that he bless and keep my family, those who are dear to me, those with whom I will have contact during the day, and all my brothers and sisters throughout this world we know and, just in case, the worlds we do not know. You see, although my educational background is heavy in science, I cannot go about life without knowing that there has to be a God in what has come to be and its evolution. I can then go about my day in peace, knowing that all I need to do at any point is simply have a brief conversation with God, asking for his help, knowing that I will have the answer at the appropriate time and place it is needed.

Reverend Garrison very thoroughly provided us with clarity in defining the activities with which we need to participate in order to receive our spiritual nurturing: the study of God's word, meditation, stress control, giving praise, worshipping, fasting, and lastly, but probably most importantly, prayer.

He reminds us that to fulfill our role as good stewards, we need nurturing from our Lord.

Allow me to take this a step further and argue that, as good stewards, we have the responsibility to nurture all parts of our lives, including ourselves. You see, God expects us to take care of ourselves, another way of saying nurture everything and everyone in your lives. Quite often, even as Christians, we forget or become selfish in our actions. We assure that we get our nurturing from the Vine and seek the support of other, like-minded souls in our journey. We get our energy boost, and we go about our lives neglecting to share that boost with others and, strangely, even ourselves. We border on becoming what I refer to as the "Bench Warming Christians" or even worse, becoming the persons who spout their religiosity to all about them but never in any way demonstrate true Christianity that will ever help recruit souls to the fold.

I believe that God first wants us to nurture ourselves. The preceding chapter in this book alludes to a number of ways in which we must nurture ourselves, including taking care of our bodies, our finances, and our spirit. But that self-nurturing also requires us to understand ourselves. We must understand what is important to us, we must develop an attitude that allows us to say each day that "I am a good person," and as I go about life, I can define what is important to me. If you talk to my friends, you will find that they will say to you that I can be very critical of myself.

But more than that, they will tell you it is not self-criticism to my detriment but, rather, a continuing review of how I do the things that I do, making judgments about how well I have completed the tasks and what I can do better the next time. In other words, I seek to learn something new each and every day of my life and to continually strive for excellence.

I do not have the illusion that I am perfect or the greatest, just that, through the blessing of our Lord, I have been given gifts and that "I can do everything through him who gives me strength" (Philippians 4:13).

We all understand that if we have been blessed to have children or work with children, we need to help build their self-esteem and love and nurture them to help them become rounded spiritual adults. Parents will tell you the all-consuming requirements of good parenting, and our author has most eloquently discussed these topics from both a spiritual and personal perspective. However, I want to remind you that a Christian (or any couple) needs to also plan to nurture their relationship. Remember, both I and Reverend Garrison have said that a part of your role in stewardship is to nurture. I am here to say that an integral part of sustaining the marriage relationship is learning to nurture each other.

This cannot be a one-way street, and the effort does not have to be great. In the marriage contract, what a couple does to make this happen will be as different from couple to couple as there are couples. The point is that it must happen. Both of you need to be partakers of the vine relationship with our Lord. As said in Matthew 6:25–34, as a couple, you need to learn to manage your stress; that is, learn to set priorities about which things are most important to you. You should not have to sweat the little things.

Have you ever sat down and just thought about the little things that are important to you in life? I, unfortunately, am the survivor of a marriage that ended after twenty-four years, a relationship in which we became lost in the forest because we could not discern the trees and take one tree at a time. As I continue to grow in my faith, I continue to grow in clarity and insight, thanks to my connection with the vine.

Three years after my divorce, I took the time to clarify what was important in a relationship for me, with my life's partner—my not-so-perfect man with a not-so-perfect woman.

As I write this and recall the list, I have had an epiphany—what I have defined in my list of basic needs are all things that are representative of what nurturing is all about. You see I didn't say tall, dark, and handsome, with a good job and excellent financial security. My list focused on what some of my friends have termed the minute stuff—touchy, feely, considerate, and doing those things that Reverend Garrison has alluded to in this work as the activities one carries out in a fulfilling Christian life. You see my epiphany, my gift of clarity from our Father, has allowed me (and hopefully you) to understand that nurturing myself, my life's partner, my children, and my sisters and brothers in life is a significant component in "the gateway to a rich and fulfilling" relationship that will allow us to "claim our inheritance."

157

Elizabeth S. Markham, PhD, RN
Associate Vice President
Academics for Nursing
Herzing University
E-mail: Emark39325@yahoo.com

CLAIMING YOUR INHERITANCE

"A GATEWAY TO A RICH AND FULFILLING LIFE"

CHAPTER TEN

CHURCH MEMBERSHIP

God's Filling Station

First, let's get one thing straight in our mind. Church will not save you.

That if you confess with your mouth, Jesus is Lord, and believe in your heart that God raised him from the dead, you will be saved.

Romans 10:9

Church, however, was not established to save anyone. Rather it was designed to serve believers, those who have confessed and accept Christ as their personal savior. It's a spiritual meeting place for those engaged in the commission that Christ gave his Church in Matthew 28:19–20 when he passed the piton to his followers to evangelize the world.

And let us consider how we may spur one another on toward love and good deeds. Let us not give up meeting together, as some are in the habit of doing, but let us encourage one another and all the more as you see the day approaching.

Hebrew 10:24–25

You know what is sad, beloved? Talking to a believer (and I use the term lightly here) who has left or refuses to go to church or connect themselves with a church. Their explanations vary, but I remember hearing: "I don't need to go to church to live a Christian life." I tell them the story of Eve and the serpent.

Being quite familiar with the story, they ask me what that has to do with them not going to church. I then expound on how Satan will take part of the truth and use it to confuse us to go his way. You see, my friend, satan is right by convincing you that you do not have to go to church to live a Christian Life, but it is virtually impossible to do, because living a Christian life involves others. I nickname the church "God's Filling Station." It is where a Christian goes to get refueled, energized, and empowered to do God's will in their lives. Christian worship does require connecting with other believers, warriors, and soldiers of the Army of the LORD.

The Reverend Dr. James F. Miller, in his book *Go Build a Church*, said: "The primary spiritual reason that people join church is not because they are enthralled with our spiritual charisma or biblical knowledge. People join because they are in need of the loving care of God. The pastor and members are conduits for this care, and 'People don't care how much we know until they know how much we care.'"

Another excuse I hear is: "I can worship at home or turn on my TV," and, yes, you can, however, you are not assembling yourselves to the body of Christ. Church is designed to strengthen your walk and enhance your knowledge of God's word, and although you have some excellent TV ministries, they are not designed for fellowship among believers, which is a requirement of being a Christian.

As a matter of fact, some TV ministers will tell you to seek a church home or place of worship at the end of their broadcast. Those programs are excellent for our sick and shut-ins, but they are not enough to equip you to do the work of the church, which each and every one of us is commissioned to do.

Rick Warren in his book, *The Purpose Driven Church*, stated: "As Christians we're called to belong, not just to believe. We are not meant to live lone-ranger lives; instead, we are to belong to Christ's family and be members of his body. Baptism is not only a symbol of salvation; it is a symbol of fellowship. It not only symbolizes our new life in Christ, it visualizes a person's incorporation into the body of Christ. It says to the world, 'This person is now one of us!' When new believers are baptized, we welcome them into the fellowship of the family of God. We are not alone. We have each other for support. I love the way Ephesians 2:19 is phrased in the Living Bible: 'You are members of God's very own family...and you belong in God's house-hold with every other Christian.' The Church exists to provide fellow-ship for believers."

Jonathan A. Dames gave another twist in his book, *Membership in Christ's Church* that gives one a sense of unity and wholeness: "It affords fellowship with those immense and towering personalities of the past. It identifies us with those who fought valiantly in the battles of life. In this sense, we are able to commune with seers, prophets, martyrs, saints, reformers, and pioneers—those immortals who chal-lenge us to do our best in our day."

Although we can read the Bible on our own and gather information and inspiration from its historical events and teaching, there is nothing like assembling with other believers; praising God with songs, hymns, and maybe even a dance; and reciting and climaxing with the preached WORD OF GOD.

At God's Filling Station, vessels of God come to be refueled to do the work of the LORD during the week. Part of the reason we are not realizing or experiencing fulfillment in our lives is that we are depend-ing on the wrong things and place to fuel or inspire us. Although church cannot save you, it is designed to do a lot for you, including keeping you on that narrow path of righteousness. How? By prayer—not just yours but by others who pray for you.

I go to church to meet other believers as we lift up the LORD in praise and worship. In E.J. Ross's *Sound Social Living*, he writes: "Religion is the expression of man's duty to his Creator. It is a social duty most fully expressed through the Church. Religious society, or the Church group, is a society formed for the social worship of the Creator. It is to be found everywhere among men, even though some of them may have lost hold of essential truth as regards the Creator and the best way to worshipping HIM, and may have a perverted notion of religion."

The word religion is derived from the Latin *religare*, to fasten or bind, and implies the bond between God and HIS creatures.

Religion is the external and social expression of this bond by means of social worship and adoration in acknowledgment of God's supreme dominion; thanksgiving in acknowledgment of HIS gifts; atonement in satisfaction for neglect of duties; and petition, which is an acknowledgment of dependence upon HIM for all that is needed.

Morality or ethics, which is an observance of the law of nature, is included in religion because the obligation to give homage and praise to God carries with it the need to obey God's laws, both those that are explicit and those that are implied by our need of an intelligent use of our nature and of the things which God has created for our use.

You cannot do all that is required at home sitting in front of your TV set. Nor can you go through the steps of worship by meditating at home by yourself. This requires fellowship, teaching, praising from songs and hymns, and hearing the challenges of the preached WORD OF GOD.

So, as you can see, church membership has its benefits. It can be a difference between the life and death of a believer. For, if a vehicle runs out of gas, it comes to a stop and cannot move until it receives more fuel. Such is the case with Christians and their relationship with the church. One cannot run this race or complete their journey without a good source for energy and empowerment—you know, that good spiritual fuel.

I attended a Home Going (funeral) service once and witnessed Elder Aaron Milton of Michigan tell a story about a great evangelist who died and went to heaven: "Heaven had an Award Ceremony where the newly arrived saints received their crown and all the gem accessories. The evangelist was excited when he entered the room and saw the array of crowns with stars, jewels, and adornments. In the middle of all the crowns was an extra-large crown with all the gems that you can imagine. Christ called the names of the saints as they bowed before

God, who placed the crown on their heads, saying: 'Well Done, Thy Good and Faithful Servant.'

"When the evangelist's name was called, he too was presented to God by our Savior but did not receive that large and special crown; however, he was grateful for what he received. After all, the LORD God was pleased.

"But then, Christ called Sister So-and-so to come up. Our evangelist was surprised to see her, for it had been so long. He had not seen her since his childhood, and he thought she had died long before him. To his surprise, she received that large and elaborate crown with all the gems and adornments. This puzzled our evangelist, so he asked Christ, what was it that she had done so well that she would receive such an award from God? After all, he had converted people in the thousands all over the world. 'Yes,' Christ replied, 'you did, and God is pleased, but she *prayed for you*!'"

You see, church membership offers so much more than just worship and praise. It's even more than bible study and getting understanding. It can be much more than friendship and fellowship. It is also where somebody, unbeknownst to you, will pray for you:

> Somebody prayed for me
> Had me on their mind
> Took the time to pray for me
> I'm so glad they prayed
> I'm so glad they prayed
> I'm so glad they prayed for me

On a more personal note, church membership was responsible for my development. As a young lad, I was labeled "special," and not in a good sense. It appeared that I tested very low academically, and the school authorities wanted to place me in a program for slow learners.

My father died when I was only nine. Living without a father was another burden that slows development and could damage a person's self-esteem. Matters got worse for me around age twelve; I felt

I had hit rock bottom in my zeal for living, and I developed a sense of hopelessness.

But, I remembered talking to my mother, who has earned another nickname from me, my "Double Mother." I called her that at times because not only did she birth me into this life, she also led me to Christ and, therefore, was the cause of my rebirth, which earned her the nickname Double Mother.

She had a tremendous amount of faith and challenged me. She said, "Well, son, you are at the age now that you can rely on the world, or on Jesus. Try my Jesus; he will fix it for you. He's a way maker and a heart fixer and a mind regulator. You just try him, and I guarantee you, he'll make a way out of no way. He'll make your way lighter and your day brighter."

Now, to tell you the truth, I had been hearing all that old-fashioned stuff at church, Sunday after Sunday after Sunday. But somehow, I was not convinced; after all, everybody saying those things was as poor as we were. But I now realized that those old, poor underachievers were exercising First Corinthians 3:6:

I planted the seed, Apollo watered it, but God made it grow.

It was a team effort: my mom planted the seed, the church family and community did the watering, and God, by the power of the Holy Spirit, did the increase.

By golly, those half-educated poor folk got the formula for enhancing self-esteem. As I look back, I realize there was a group of geniuses at Starlight Temple of Truth, for they learned how to tap into the resource and teach their children how to connect to a force, a power outside of themselves.

It used to anger me when the pastor or leader would get up during the Service and just announce: "We will be led in prayer by Master Garrison." I would be in shock! They would have said nothing to me beforehand or the Sunday before, when I could have practiced like children and their parents insist on today. No way! I would glance at my mother, and she would have that look on her face that said, "If you want to keep breathing, you will get up and pray and represent this family like you were trained to do." What a cruel thing to do to an eight-to-sixteen-year-old kid. But, as I look back on it, I realize they too were buying into my self-esteem, building it up, and the more I participated in church, the more confident I became.

They did not allow me to hang my head and take the excuse that I was an introvert or that I was shy or just had a quiet spirit. No, it did not work in that little ghetto, nondenominational church; everybody participated, from the youngest to the oldest, and not one person was allowed to display a low self-esteem. That's why, out of that neighbor-hood, came a lot of high achievers who surprised a good many folk.

You see, church played another role in my mother's life and ours. She found not only refuge from a world of hopelessness but a great source of support in raising the six of us without a husband or a good job that afforded her a good lifestyle and social status for her and her children. She was able to find support and help raising us, not to men-tion an enormous amount of love.

Today, now that I am good and grown, I still reflect on my childhood in that run-down church in the ghetto and how we all became family and gave unconditional love to each other.

I guess it explains how my sister Carrie now plays piano for her church each and every Sunday, my brother Tim plays the violin for his church, my brother Paul is a trustee, and my sister Ina is in the choir. It also explains why I became a preacher. They made me do it. I remem-ber after I prayed (which children had to do at our church, impromptu) or summarized a Sunday-school lesson, those old folk would come up to me and say: "Boy, you are going to be a preacher one day, you just watch." They were crazy! No, way Jose. Guess what, they knew what they were talking about.

But, it was not just that church. Later in life, I served in the mili-tary during a time when veterans were not respected much. When I was discharged from service, my two siblings had joined the great and historic Bethel. I was intimidated by the church because of its size and the prominent people who were part of the membership. I followed my siblings there, but with a slightly negative attitude. One day, a gentleman named Clarence Jones approached me and challenged me. He noticed that I was not comfortable there but had very little knowledge of the Methodist faith. So, he had me read the mission of the church. Wow, I was hooked. The mission of the church said all the things I thought a church should stand for, and to this day, I am grateful for his evangelism. Now, Clarence was not a preacher, just a member of the church.

Then I met a young lady named Lidia Hibbert, who I call my mother in the teaching ministry. Why? Because she was the one who made me stop and listen to God.

She approached me one day and asked me to teach Sunday school. I wasn't too sure what that meant, so I asked her what the qualifications were. Well, at that time there were none. So, as I taught, I wrote and made notes until I submitted an idea of certifying Sunday school teachers.

Later I met Paul Billingslea, who introduced me to the Reverend Dr. Kenneth Hill. Dr. Hill further developed the work and published it, and my idea became the certification system for church schoolteachers, superintendents, and has grown to include directors of Christian education.

Then came the Reverend Maurice J. Higginbothan, who was determined to make me a preacher because I was still fighting the concept. You see, I was an accountant with my own tax-consulting business, which was a long way from the pulpit. But, guess what, he won. How he did it was another story.

God has placed so many people in my life that have made a difference, too numerous for me to mention. That's when my life took on a new meaning and new direction. You see, my friend, I am not just talking about a "pie in the sky and the sweet by and by." I'm talking about having life and having it more abundantly. This is where I became somebody; I got the acceptance, the love, the spiritual nurturing, and plenty of HUGS.

Everyone was meant to share
God's all abiding love and care;
HE saw that we would need to know
A way to let these feelings show...
SO GOD MADE HUGS

Jill Wolf

As a pastor in Wisconsin, I have incorporated HUGS as part of my ministry:

Helping those in need
Unifying the community through our ministering to others
Growing by teaching God's word
Serving with our Spiritual gifts

But then I literally have our members hug each other every Sunday. Now, in this present society, some folk are reluctant to hug, so I announce if you do not want to hug, just extend your hand for a shake, and if you don't want to touch, then just give a nice warm Chinese bow, but, by all means, greet at least twenty-one people today. Why twenty-one? Well, I read an article some time ago that said if a person gets three hugs in a day; it could actually change their attitude. So, I want them all to have a good attitude for that entire week.

Well, I'm not sure about that, but it sure looks right when I see my congregation greeting each other every Sunday.

Church membership is important for all believers because it has been established by Christ to enhance our spiritual growth, fellowship, support, and service. But, even more than that, I am a living witness that it can actually change, develop, and produce a life out of hopelessness. God met my family there and transformed us, which made all the difference in the world to us. We lived in a place that was surrounded by what looked like failure and with no chance of success or, in some cases, survival, yet through God's grace and willing believers, we all

167

found hope, love, acceptance, and that helping hand that made me who I am today.

There is nothing like it, and I recommend if you don't have a church home, please find one.

My mom went a little further with her sales presentation; she explained that "you can't measure God's blessings with a worldly yard-stick." She asked me if I ever went hungry.

"No," I had to admit, even though I remember us running out of money many times.

"Were you ever sick? Had any deformities?"

Well, other than what the school was telling me, no. She went on and questioned me on all the necessities of life and had me look at our neighbors around us. She opened my eyes to see that, although things seemed a little grim in the midst of the public housing and all the crime, suffering, and hopelessness that we saw, our family, the "Holy-Roly Goody, Goody Two-Shoes," which some called us, were doing pretty good. She then told me that it was because she made a choice for her family and brought us up in such a way that God will bless us, despite our surroundings, and that each and every one of her children was somebody special. She told me that God had a blessing for me but that I needed to claim it.

Wow, I stopped feeling sorry for myself, and my value of myself started to increase. I cannot tell you that things started to change over-night for me, it took her talking to me a few times more, but, eventually, I understood I had to claim what God had in store for me; it wouldn't just drop in my lap, but it was there for the claiming.

Only the church is where a believer can assemble with others and experience the awesome spiritual uplifting that you can only receive during worship service. From the very beginning of the service, as we recite the "Call to Worship," we open our hearts, minds, and souls to invoke the Holy Spirit into our presence. It is a great feeling when we hear the choir sing anthems like "Come Let Us Worship the Lord in the Beauty of Holiness," "Guide Me O Thy Great Jehovah," "Great Is Thy

Faithfulness," or a song I got from an old preacher, "Down through the Years, God's Been Good to Me."

We can also worship God in dance, recital, and other forms of expression. Even bringing my tithes and offering is a blessing and honor. When you leave the church, you are ready to go another week, fighting on the battlefield and equipped to run the race.

"It will be your first step toward
'Claiming Your Inheritance.'"

CHAPTER ELEVEN

ESTEEM

Developing Your Self-Esteem

We discussed the importance of a positive attitude, which is a by-product of faith, in Chapter Eight. However, developing a positive attitude is not easy if one has been battling with low self-esteem. This chapter is an attempt to combat negativity and suggest ways to help build self-esteem, not just for ourselves but, more importantly, for our offspring and those depending on us for their personal development.

The Reverend Jesse Jackson had a saying that I would like to paraphrase: "It's not your aptitude that determines your altitude in life; rather, it's your attitude." I have read many stories and biographies of people who have achieved greatness in life. Most of them experienced a great deal of failures as well. But, there was something within them that did not allow them to quit or give up. Reverend Jackson was speaking to a group of inner-city high-school kids when he inspired them to dare to dream. He reminded them of the many people in history who were not blessed with the brightest of minds but a good dose of positive attitude and self-esteem. He shared with them that their aptitude was God given to equip them to accomplish anything they envisioned, but it was their attitude that would empower them to carry out and realize their dreams.

But, how do you think positive about yourself when surrounded by negative forces? How does one develop faith in the midst of hopelessness and when you feel helpless and powerless about your situation or worse, those closest to you are pessimistic about their future and yours?

Self-esteem is one of the most important ingredients for success or any form of positive achievement in life. What if I told you that you are a vessel of God and that God has chosen to work through you for certain blessings, not just for you but also as a blessing for others.

Henry Ford once said: "Whether you believe you can or you can't, you are probably right." Beloved, that's because the mind is a powerful source between our ears. It can actually dictate if we live or die.

There was a hobo who hopped on a freight train one night. As he closed the door behind him, it locked, and he could not unfasten the latch. As he looked around, he noticed that the car was marked "Refrigerator Car." As he felt his body getting cold, he crawled in a corner of the car and started writing his last words: "Getting colder by the minute, I feel myself getting sleepy as my blood runs cold. I feel my heart pumping slower, it won't be long now. Good-bye cruel world, I never really felt a part anyway. Now I will get my final rest."

That next morning they found the body of the hobo in the broken refrigerator car; it was being shipped for repair. But, the hobo had already programmed his mind for defeat and death, and once he had made up his mind, very little could have changed it.

Some of us, like that hobo, have accepted that our life will not amount to anything, so as Henry Ford stated, you are right. Not that God meant it to be, but we programmed it to be. I have met some very gifted people in my life, and some aren't any better off than the character Forrest Gump because of their defeatist attitude. Like the servant that buried his talent, they just gave up on themselves and allowed Satan to enter their minds to convince them that they cannot achieve. You have to use it or you will lose it, but God will still reckon with you. The question is, "Will God be proud of you; or disappointed in you?"

Self-esteem can influence our attitude in life, which directly affects how far we go in life and our quality of life. Have you ever met someone that seems to be so gifted and wondered why they weren't happy or fulfilled? There are some real bright, intelligent, and gifted people out there that will not amount to much because something has happened in their past that has stifled them. I remember meeting a young man who graduated from an Ivy League school. He possessed a very high IQ and could read a two hundred–page book in a matter of a couple of hours. The young man could quote Shakespeare and the psychological theories of Sigmund Freud. But, his confidence level was so low that he did not have the courage to venture out of his comfort zone. As a result, he lives a somewhat comfortable life because of his supreme intelligence, but he is also quite miserable because his mind is constantly in need of challenges.

Maybe something happened in his childhood. I have read many articles that suggest that what a child is exposed to and taught in their formative years will shape that child for a lifetime. Although genes do play a part in our personalities, many psychologists will attest to that, I believe your exposure and upbringing have a greater impact and influence.

How many times have we heard children being adopted from families of what society may call losers? But, those children are exposed to love, nurturing, and a healthy atmosphere, only to grow and excel into wonderful productive citizens—a far cry from their biological beginnings.

To paraphrase from Norman Vincent Peale's book *You Can If You Think You Can*:

"If we develop greater appreciation of the immense resources built into the mind, we can do amazing things—even greater than we dare to imagine. What a person can be and what a person can do is largely determined by the degree of self-limitation he mentally imposes on himself. If he imagines himself on a restrictive level, the flow of resources from the mind will be reduced and maintained at a trickle of the full potential. If, on the contrary, his image of himself and his possibilities is comprehensive and exact, the volume of resource power from the mind will be correspondingly larger. A certain degree of boldness is required of the individual who wishes to make more of himself or herself. Boldness is an activator of power from the mind."

Can you imagine having that level of self-confidence along with Christ's teachings?

I tell you the truth, anyone who has faith in me will do what I have done. He will do even greater things than these, because I am going to the Father. And I will do whatever you ask in my name, so that the Son may bring glory to the Father. You may ask me for anything in my name, and I will do it.

John 14:12–14

You have the power to do great things if you first believe in yourself, and, second, believe in Christ, who will empower you to accomplish what you need through the Holy Spirit. Christ went further to explain how you can achieve great things in Chapter 15 of the gospel of John:

I am the true vine, and my Father is the gardener, HE cuts off every branch in me that bears no fruit, while every branch that does bear fruit he prunes so that it will be even more fruitful. You are already clean because of the word I have spoken to you. Remain in me, and I will remain in you. No branch can bear fruit by itself; it must remain in the vine. Neither can you bear fruit unless you remain in me.

John 15:1–4

The key is being connected to the vine. That's your power source. This is how we soar; this is how we can accomplish great things.

To claim your inheritance as an achiever, you must first understand and develop a good self-esteem, which is self-value. How do you feel about yourself? No matter what your family, school, or the world says about you, you are special. You may not be a rock star, great athlete, or singer, but you are someone special because God made you special. How? By adopting you into a special family of believers called Christians. All you really need to do is accept the adoption. Once you do that, the stage is set for you to do your thing. Once you find your blessing(s) or gift(s), God has provided guidelines, given by Christ, on how to discover, perfect, and use your gift(s). But you need to believe that God loves you just as much as any other person in the world and has made us all unique and special just for the service that only you can give.

Then, my friend, you must learn how to stay connected to the source, to the vine, to the power center that God has established for you and me: Christ.

Whenever I got in a slump and indulged in my self-pity party, my mom would have me face the mirror and go through what appeared to be a military chant: "I am God's Child, and I can be what he wants me to be and whatever I want to be." Sometimes I would not say it loud enough for her, and she would say: "Louder, I want to hear you" or "I am not convinced that you mean it, boy." I sometimes thought she didn't love me like the others, for she was so very hard on me, but I realize it was because I probably had the lowest esteem, and she just wouldn't have it. So, she would not let me give up or rest. She was determined to make something out of me and would seek help from anyone and anywhere. If she saw a man of positive means and character, she would turn to me and say, "Look at him, talk to him, study him, and you can be like him. Boy, you're going to be somebody one day, just keep on trusting in the Lord."

In her own way, she developed a Home Support Network with us kids. I had no idea what she was doing, and to be truthful with you, I'm not sure if she knew, but it knitted our family close and trained us to be loving and supportive and to lift each other's esteem. She would never allow us to call each other degrading names or belittle each other. She really got on us if she overheard us call another sibling stupid or dumb. She would stop what she was doing and read the riot act to us.

We could not fight each other (now that was a hard one for my two older brothers), but by the time Tim and I were teenagers, it was well ingrained in us. We could only use supportive words to our brothers and sisters. She would always remind us that we were representing the Garrison family in everything we did and that we must do that to the best of our ability. Not only were we expected to have a good self-esteem, but we were taught to have good family esteem as well, and that meant loving and supporting each other.

From her teachings, my brother Marshall (who was the second oldest) took the position of sibling mentor after our father died, and his words of guidance were surprisingly wise. Marshall really was the spearhead of Chapters Four and Ten, a very wise man with an unassuming lifestyle. I remember him always telling me: "Little bro, never hang around somebody that knows less than you. Pick your friends like you are picking your future. You want to go somewhere in life, hang around with somebody that's going places." His favorite saying to me was: "Bro, you're different, and that's good. This is a competitive world, and you got to be different to be better, so you can't be like everybody else."

He and my sister Carrie became my great supporters in each and everything I tried to do. If any of us were attacked or jumped on, which was a common thing in public housing, we all were involved. That little lady did a marvelous job on us, and it took her explaining to me that I was somebody in God's eye and that God did not forget me when handing out gifts, talents, and blessing. She would tell you today that she didn't know how she was about to produce four out of six kids with college degrees from the public housing.

But I know how she did it. It is because she said it all the time: "If it had not been for the LORD on my side, where would I be?" (Which was a song she often sang)? Another one was "I will trust in the Lord."

As a result of all the drills and esteem building, my oldest brother Paul became my hero. He really set the stage for us, as the oldest sibling often does. He started off as a firefighter and was credited for saving many lives and earning citations and awards. He eventually became chief of training, and, after retirement, was appointed director of public safety in another major city. One of my sisters sang for the Michigan Opera, while my other brother was a member of the US Army Boxing Team.

I am so proud of my family and what God has done for us, but, I better stop now, because my mother will get on me for bragging. But,

I think she knows by now that I am not bragging, rather, I am testifying on what God has done and can do for you. So often she told us not to brag, just be thankful for what God has done through you.

On the other hand, I mentioned earlier that I spearheaded a Homeless Program at my home church. I remember talking to a young lady who appeared to have a very impressive background. She was a degreed nurse with some post-graduate studies under her belt. I could not help myself in asking her what happened, how she came to a place of homelessness; after all, she can walk into anyone's hospital and get a job pretty much on the spot, so why in the world was she going from homeless shelter to homeless shelter?

She acknowledged that she was well educated and had accomplished impressive academic goals, but she always struggled with low self-esteem that was implanted in her by her parents, who failed to support her aspirations. She fell in love with a truck driver who supported her in everything she did, but he could not keep a job because of multiple traffic tickets and points. They lost everything, including their home, but because he loved her and she loved him, she chose to live with him in homeless shelters with their two children, rather than to go back home to her professional family where she never felt loved, supported, or encouraged.

What a tragic story; what a terrible way to go through life with your own parents not accepting or encouraging you. Now, you would like to think that having parents who were achievers themselves would be enough for her to keep her head up, but esteem does not elevate itself, it must be nurtured, and the most effective way or source to nurture esteem or destroy it is by the ones you love and can most identify with.

This is something that I would like to share with you, beloved. No matter where you are in life or your circumstances, surroundings, or economic status, God loves you and has made provisions for you. Now, if you are a parent and don't know what to do that can help your children along in this tough world, I recommend my mother's Family Support Network plan, and you can start by just looking your child in the eye and saying:

"I LOVE YOU!"

Then, routinely have them look at themselves in the mirror and have them to say, shout, and repeat over and over again one of Jesse Jackson's favorite sayings:

"I am somebody, for I am God's child. I am beautiful and I am blessed because God made me that way. I can and I will achieve all the God has placed in me!"

To you who do not have believing parents or parents at all, I am writing this for you, beloved. God wants you successful, God wants you happy, and God wants you to overcome and find a way to "Claim Your Inheritance" that is promised to you through Jesus the Christ.

Veronique Dupree Chastain said it best in her book *Possible*:

"You may be thinking there is no earthly way you will make it through. There may be no earthly way, if you simply look at the finite facts of this world, but beyond this finite world there is an infinite universe with infinite possibilities. Try listening for and to your own inner voice. Ask and actually expect to get an answer. Choose to think it is possible; believe it is possible; and come to know that anything is possible!"

R. Kelly recorded a song, although secular, that carries a very strong spiritual meaning. The words are:

I used to think that I could not go on
And life was nothing but an awful song
But now I know the meaning of true love
I'm leaning on the everlasting arms

If I can see it, then I can do it
If I just believe it, there's nothing to it

I believe I can fly
I believe I can touch the sky
I think about it every night and day
Spread my wings and fly away

I believe I can soar
I see me running through that open door
I believe I can fly
I believe I can fly
I believe I can fly

So, beloved, claim your blessing, and claim your rightful inheritance. Just, believe that God intended for you to be all that he has put in you. So, beloved, just

Reach out and grab it!

·

CLAIMING YOUR INHERITANCE

"A GATEWAY TO A RICH AND FULFILLING LIFE"

INDEX

A

Aaron Milton (Heaven's Award
  Ceremony) 162
Ability to produce wealth
  (Deuteronomy 8:18) 56
Accident in space (the creation) 12
Achieving,
 Greater than Christ 13
Adolf Hitler, 2
 Aryan Race Philosophy 2
Agape' 5
Albert Einstein 138
Allen, Bishop Richard 137
American Institute for Cancer
  Research 44-45
Amelia Clabots 43
Aminos,
 Liquid 36
Amos Chester VI
Ann Romney 2
Apostles
 Calling of God (Ephesians 4:11-
  14) 140
Arnold Schmidt, "Closer to the
  Source" 50

Atheist 17
ATTITUDE, 131
 Connecting to the power source
  (The Vine) 174-175
 Determine your altitude (Rev.
  Jesse Jackson) 171
Authority,
 Spiritual 22
Avoid Debt at all cost 77

B

Baby,
Lack of mother's love 2
Bag Lady (Rich Man – Poor
  Woman) 9
Barack Obama 127

Barrower,
Servant to the Leader (Proverbs
  22:7) 76
Be a servant with a purpose
  11-31
Being connected (John 14: 12-14)
  174
Ben Carson 138

Benny Hen 137
Bill Gates 125, 127
Billingslea, Paul 166
Billy Graham 137
Big Tip (Pregnant young woman)
    26-27
Bing Bang theory 11
Bishops,
    Gregory Gerald McKinley
        Ingram 95
    John Richard Bryant 107-108,
        137
    Richard Allen 137
Blessings,
    Measure 67
Bleeding woman 99
Blind,
    Beggar 99-100
Building a Church
    Dr. James F. Miller 160
Blood Pressure 35, 46
Body,
    Mass Index 38
    Temple of God (I Corinthians
        3:16-17, 6:19-20) 33-34
Boy Scout,
    Saying, "I would rather see a
        sermon, than to hear one"
        15, 25
Brother,
    Who is my brother 7-8
Bryant, Bishop John Richard
    107-108, 137

Bryant, Cecelia Williams 30,
    71-73, 83-84
Buddhist 17
Budget,
    Avoid debt 77-87
    Establish your budget 71-77
    Living under your means 71-73
Buffet, Warren 125
But, the greatest of these is Love
    (1 Corinthians 13: 1-13) 1-9

C
Call to Worship 168
Calories,
    Burning 39-40
    Counting 40
    Diet 39
    Exercise 38
Capitalistic Society 53
Carlton, Linda (Reactive Article)
    88-89
Carolyn Butts Garrison VI
Carolyn Davis 95
Carson, Dr. Ben 138
Cecelia Williams Bryant 30,
    71-73, 83-84
Challenges of Jesus 149-152
    Wilderness experience
        (Matthew 4: 1-11) 150
Chastain, Veronique Dupree
    (Possible) 178
Chemical explosion or imbalance
    11

China Study (T. Collin Campbell) 42

Christian society 110

Cholesterol,
  Diet 37, 47
  LDL/HDL 37-38, 47

Chosen People (I Peter 2:9) 67, 138

Christian Economics 70-75, 102

Christian Society 110

Church
  "Go Build a Church" (James F. Miller) 160
  Membership 17
  "Membership in Christ's Church" (Jonathan A. Dames) 17, 160
  "Purpose driven Church" (Rich Warren) 160

CHURCH MEMBERSHIP 159

Cleopatra and Mark Anthony 4

Connected,
"I am the True Vine" (John 15:1-8) 98, 174

To the Vine (John 14: 12-14) 174

Cox, David (Reactive Article) 86-88

Creator can to a SHE 15

D

Dalai Lama 53-54

David Cox (Reactive Article) 86-88

Debt,
  American Debt Adviser 76
  Avoid 77-86
  Eliminate debt 81-83

Get and stay out of debt pledge 78-81

Degree,
  I got my degree (Story of a Young College Graduate) 23
  Love 3

Developing your self esteem 171-174

Devilish Boys 140

Diet 35-37, 42-45

Divine resource 69, 98, 114, 174

Doctor,(Medical/PhD)
  Ben Carson 138
  Buettner, Dan 43
  Campbell, T. Collin 42-43
  Charles Dew 119, 138
    Johnson, LaDonna (Reactive Article) 46
    Kemp, Juanita (Reactive Article) 50-51
    Markham, Elizabeth (Reactive Article) 155-158
    Nguyen, Nhung V. (Reactive Article) 47-49

Doing the right thing

Integrity 103

Involving others (Galatians 6:10) 128

Dolly Parton (What's love got to do with it) 6

Dominican Republic (Youth Mission Trip) 30-31

Don't Quit (Poem) 93

Don't Worry (Matthew 6:25-34) 147

Doris M. Akers (You Can't Beat God's Giving) 63

Double Mother 164

Dr. Zhivago 4

Dwight Nichols (God's Plan for your Finance) 66-67

E

E.J. Ross (Sound Social Living) 161

ECONOMICS 53

Eliminate debt 81-83

Elizabeth Markham (Reactive Article) 155-158

Elohim can be a SHE 15

Eros 3-4

ESTEEM 171

Esther & Mordecai 135-136

Evangelist,
   Billy Graham 137

Calling (Ephesians 4:11-14) 140
   Carolyn Davis 95-96

Exercise 38,44

F

Faith 99, 102, 117-118
   Positive attitude 135- 139

Fasting
   Prayer & Fasting (Matthew 17: 14-21) 27-28, 96
   Resilience 91-111

Father
   Creator (Genesis 1: 27-28 11-13

God/Jehovah/Elliham/Yahweh 14-15 Loving father 23

Five-fold Ministry 140

Food, Inc. 4

Footprints (poem) 29

Freight Train 172

Fruit of the Spirit (Galatians 5: 16-25) 16

G

Gambling v/s investing 59-61

Gates, Bill 125, 127

Gatewood, Rev. Dr. L.A. IX

George Washington 138

George Washington Carver 138

Gift of God
   (Ephesians 4:11-14) 140

Gift of the Spirit
   (Ephesians 4:11-14) 140

Give
   An account (Matthew 25: 14-30, Luke 12:48, Romans 14:12) 114 116 from the heart (2 Corinthians 9:7) 65 and it will be given to you (Luke 6:38) 65 honor the Lord with your first fruit and crop (Proverbs 3:9-10) 66

God's
   Anointing (Ephesians 4:11-14) 140
   Blessings (Luke 6: 38) 65-68
   Calling (Ephesians 4:11-14) 140
   Can be a SHE 15

184

Is a spirit 15
Plans for your Finances (Dwight
   Nichols) 66-67
Purpose 11, 116, 164
Want's you out of debt 76, 83
Good Samarian
   (Luke 10: 29-35) 8
   Young poor man 26-27
Graham, Evangelist Billy 137
Great Commission (Matthew 28:
   18-20) 20-21
Greed
   Parable of the Greedy Rich
      Farmer (Luke 12: 16-21) 119
Gregory Gerald McKinley
   Ingram 95

H
H.I.V./A.I.D.S. 107
Harriet Tubman 138
HEALTH 33
Hen, the Reverend Benny 137
Henry Ford, Attitude 172
Hibert, Lydia VI, 166
Higginbothan, Marice J. 166
High Blood Pressure 35
His image 11-12
Hobo on a freight train 172
Holy Roly Goody, Goody, Two
   Shoes 168
Homosexuality,
   (Genesis 19:1-13) 106
   (Leviticus 18:22) 106
   (Romans 1:21-27) 107

Honor the Lord (Proverbs 3:9-10)
   66
Hugs (Jill Wolf) 167
Human Development (Robert V.
   Kail and John C. Cavanaugh) 91

I
I am God's child 178
I am the true Vine (John 15: 1-8)
   25-26, 98, 174
I Believe I Can Fly (R. Kelly)
   178-179
I can do all things through Christ
   (Philippians 4: 13) 135
I got my degree 23-24
I rather see a sermon than to
   hear one (unknown Boy Scout)
   15,25
Image, His/God's/Divine 11-12
Ingram, Bishop Gregory Gerald
   McKinley 95
INSPIRATION 1
INTEGRITY 103
Invest/Investments/Investing
   Like playing the lottery 59-61
   God's servant 73
   Chart 75

J
James F. Miller (Go Build A
   Church) 160
Jehovah can be a SHE 15
Jesus in the wilderness (Matthew
   4: 1-11) 150

Jill Wolf (So God Made Hugs) 167
Job (Job 1: 1-5, 6-8) 153-154
Johnson, La Donna, MD (Reactive
    Article) 46
Joseph (Genesis 39) 152
Juanita P. Kemp, PhD (Reactive
    Article) 51

K
Kenneth Hill 166
King, Rev. Dr. Martin Luther 137

L
Lack of Self-Control (Proverbs
    25:28) 133
La Donna J. Johnson, MD
    (Reactive Article) 46
Leprosy
    Man (Luke 17: 11-19) 101-102
    Men (2 Kings 7: 3-8) 134-135
Life/living
    Abundant, fuller, greater life
        (John 10:10b) 14, 15
    Life Style (standard of living)
        43-45
    Living sacrifice (Romans 12:
        1-2) 131
    Living under your means 71-73
Linda Carlton (Reactive Article)
    88-89
Liquid Aminos 36
Little pray, little power 95
Lottery v/s investments 59-61
Love

Agape 5
Ann Romney 2
Each other (John 15: 9-13) 7
Eros 3
Greater love has no man ....
    (Luke 15: 9-13) 7
    Greek 3
    Human 2, 4-5, 177-178
    Lack of Love 2, 177
    Love Never Fails (I Corinthians
        13:1-13) 1
    Michelle Obama 2
    No greater love (John 15: 9-13) 7
    Phileos 4
    Stauros/Storge 4
Luther, Martin 137
Lydia Hibbert VI, 166

M
M.I.T. Experience (Bishop John
    Richard Bryant) 137
Man
    Leprosy (Luke 17: 11-19)
        101-102
    Parable of the Rich Young Ruler
        (Mark 10: 17-27) 57 Parable
        of the Greedy Rich Farmer
        (Luke 12: 16-21) 119
    Story of the Poor Young Man
        26-27
Markham, Elizabeth, PhD.
    (Reactive Article) 155-158
Martine Luther 137
Martin Luther King, Jr. 137

Marvin Sapp (Never Would Have
   Made It) 93-94
Maurice J. Higginbothan VI, 166
Meditation 145
Men
   Leprosy (2 Kings 7: 3-8)
      134-135
   Parable of the Greedy Rich
      Farmer (Luke 12: 16-21)
      119
Parable of the Talents (Matthew
   25: 14-30) 113-114
Milton, Elder Aaron (Heaven's
   Award Ceremony) 162
Mind
Renewing of your mind (Roman
   12: 1-2) 131
Money
   Love of Money (Mark 10:
      17-27) 57
   (I Timothy 6:10a) 59
   Parable of the Greedy Rich
      Farmer (Luke 12: 16-21) 119
Mordecai & Esther (Esther)
   135-136
Much pray, much power 95
Muslim 16-17

N
Nazirite (Sampson) 152-153
Never Would Have Made It
   (Marvin Sapp) 93-94
Nguyen, Nhung V, ND Lac
   (Reactive Article) 47-49

Nhung V. Nguyen, ND Lac
   (Reactive Article) 47-49
NIA 11
No prayer, no power 94-95
Norman Vincent Peale (You can if
   you think you can) 173
NUTURE 143

O
Oprah Winfrey 125, 127
Obama, President Barack 127

P
Parables
   Don't worry about your life
      (Matthew 6: 25-34) 146-147
   Good Samarian (Luke 10:
      29-35) 8
   Rich man who build a bigger
      barn for more (Luke 12:
      16-21) 119
   The sheep and the Goats
      (Matthew 25: 31-40) 129
   The Talents (Matthew25:
      14-30) 113-114
   True Vine (John 15: 1-8) 25
Pastors
   (Ephesians 4: 11-14) 140
Paul Billingslea 166
Peale, Norman Vincent (You can if
   you think you can) 173
Phileos 4
Plant
   The seed 164

Pledge to be out of debt 78
Poems
   To My Sons (Start Climbing) VIII
   Two Natures 16, 97
   Footprints 29
   Don't Quit 93
   Hugs (Jill Wolf) 167
Poor
   Woman and two devilish
     boys 140
   Young Man and Rich woman
     26-27
Positive thinking
   Attitude 131, 171
   Greater thing you can do (John
     14: 12-14) 174
   Hobo is a freight train 172
   Power of the mind (Henry
     Ford) 172
   Renewing of your mind
     (Roman 12: 1-2) 131
You can if you think you can
   (Norman Vincent Peale) 173
Possibility/Possible (Veronique
   Dupree Chastain) 178
Power
   Connect to the vine 174-175
   Of the mind 131-133, 171-175
   Source 174-175
   Spiritual 25
   To heal (prayer and fasting,
     Matthew 17: 14-21) 27-28
   Witness 27, 29
Praise 100, 102

And Worship 148
Prayer and Fasting 149
Prayer/Pray/Praying
   (Matthew 4: 1-11) 150
     (Matthew 6: 16-18) 149
     (Matthew 17: 14-21) 27-28
     Pop-Tart Prayer (Evangelist
     Carolyn Davis) 95 Somebody
     prayed for me 163
   Pastor's pray for brother
     promotion 122-123
Pregnant young woman 26-27
President Barack Obama 127
Priesthood (I Peter 2:9) 67
Prophets (Ephesians 4: 11-14)
   140
Prosper
   Achieving 137-139, 164, 174
   In good health (3 John, v2) 35
Proverbs
   "I rather see a sermon than
     to hear one" (unknown Boy
     Scout) 15,25
A man who feels he has all he
   needs just because rich 86
A man who lack self-control
   (Proverbs 25: 28) 133
Boy Scout proverb ("I rather
   see a sermon than to hear
   one") 25
Honor the Lord with your
   wealth (Proverbs 3: 9-10) 66
Now consider the ant, you
   sluggard; consider its ways

and be wise (Proverbs 6:
6-11) 61
The borrower is servant to the
lender (Proverbs 22: 7) 76
Purpose 116
NIA 11, 116
Renewing of your mind
(Roman 12: 1-2) 133

Q

R

R. Kelly (I Believe I Can Fly)
178-179
Reactive Articles
David Cox, CFP (Economics)
86-88
Elizabeth Markham, PhD
(NUTURE) 155-158
Juanita P. Kemp, PhD (Health)
50-51
LaDonna J. Johnson, M.D.
(Health) 46
Linda Garrison-Carlton, C.P.A,
(Economics) 88-89
Nhung V. Nguyen, ND Lac
(Health) 47-49
Reconciliation (2 Corinthians 5:
18-20) 29-31
Refrigerator Car (Freight train) 172
Renewing of your mind (Roman
12: 1-2) 131
Republican

Convention (Ann Romney
talked of Love) 2
Ron Paul 60-61
RESILIENCE 91
Retirement
Ten percent to God's Servant
(Yourself) 73
Plan for the future 74-76
Chart 75
Reverend
Aaron Milton 162
Amos Chester VI
Benny Hen 137
Billy Graham 137
Cecelia Williams Bryant
30-31, 71
E. J. Ross (Sound Social Living)
161
James F. Miller (Go Build A
Church) 160
Jesse Jackson 171
Jonathan A. Dames
(Membership in Christ
Church) 17, 161
Kenneth Hill 166
L. A. Gatewood IX
Martin Luther King, Jr. 137
Martin Luther 137
Maurice J. Higginbothan VI, 166
Paul Billingslea VI, 166
Rick Warren (Purpose Driven
Church) 160
Rudi Gelsey 110-111
Rich

Abundantly (John 10: 10b) 14
Rich Man – Poor Woman 9
Rich man who build a bigger barn
    for more (Luke 12: 16-21) 119
    Abraham (Genesis 14: 22-23) 58
Rich woman and poor young man
    26-27
    Young Ruler 57
Rick Warren (Purpose Driven
    Church) 160
Robbing God (Malachi 3: 8-10)
    64-65
Romeo and Juliet 4
Ron Paul (Confederation
    currency) 60-61

S
Salt
    Diet 36, 45
    You are the salt of the earth
        (Matthew 5:13) 139
Samaritan
    (Luke 10: 29-35) 8
Sampson 152-153
Satan temps Jesus in the
    wilderness (Matthew 4: 1-11,
    Luke 4: 1-13) 150
Satan left Jesus until an
    opportune time (Luke 4: 13)
    150-152
Screening
    Test 40-41
Scripture
    OLD TESTAMENT

2 Kings 4: 1-7 (The widow and
    oil) 70
2 Kings 7: 3-8 (Survival of the
    Lepers) 134-135
Daniel 3: 16-18 (Do what is
    right) 109
Deuteronomy 8:18 (For it is HE
    who give you the ability to
    produce wealth) 56
Esther 4: 13-14 (You have come
    to royal position for such a
    time as this) 136
Esther 4: 11 (Esther and
    Mordecai) 136
Genesis 1: 24-28 (HE created
    him; male and female, HE
    created them) 11, 105
Genesis 14: 18-20 (Then Abram
    gave him a tenth of every-
    thing) 62
Genesis 14: 22-23 (You will
    never be able to say "I made
    Abram rich") 58
Genesis 19: 1-13 (Sodom and
    Gomorrah) 106
Job 1: 1-5 (He was the greatest
    man among all the people of
    the East) 154
Job 1: 6-8 (Have you consid-
    ered my servant Job?) 153
Leviticus 18: 22
    (Homosexuality) 106
Malachi 3: 8-10 (Will a man rob
    God?) 64-65

Proverbs 3: 9-10 (Honor the Lord with your wealth) 66

Proverbs 6: 6-11 (go to the ant, you sluggard; consider its ways and be wise) 61

Proverbs 22: 7 (The borrower is servant to the lender) 76

Proverbs 25: 28 (A man who lack self-control) 133

Psalms 35:27 (Let the LORD be exalted) 135

Psalms 84: 10 (I would rather be a doorkeeper in the house of God) 149

Psalms 122: 1-2 (Let us go to the house of the LORD) 148

NEW TESTAMENT

1 Corinthians 3: 6 (I planted the seed, Apollo watered it, God made it grow) 164

1 Corinthians 3: 16-17 (Don't you know that you yourselves are God's temple) 33

1 Corinthians 6: 19-20 (your body is a temple of the Holy Spirit) 34, 45

I Corinthian 13: 1-13 (And now I show you the most excellent way) 1

I Corinthian 13: 1-13 (Love never fails) 1

1 John 4: 20-21 (If anyone says, "I love God," yet hate his brother) 127

1 Peter 2: 9 (But you are a chosen people) 67, 138

1 Timothy 6:10a (For the love of money is a root of all kinds of evil) 59

2 Corinthians 12: 10 (For when I am weak, then I am strong) 95

2 Corinthians 5: 18-20 (We are therefore Christ's ambassadors) 30

2 Corinthians 9:7 (God loves a cheerful giver) 65

2 Timothy 2: 15-16 (Study to show thyself approved unto God) 144

3 John, verse 2 (I pray that you may enjoy good health) 35

Acts 1:8 (But you will receive power when the Holy Spirit comes on you) 15

Acts 19: 13-16 (Jesus I know, and I know Paul, but who are you?) 22

Ephesians 4: 11-14 (Apostles, Prophets, Evangelist, Pastors and Teachers) 140

Galatians 5: 16-25 (Fruits of the Spirit) 16

Galatians 6: 10 (let us do good to all people) 128

Hebrew 10: 24-25 (Let us not give up meeting together) 159

John 2: 12-19 (Jesus challenged by the Jewish Leadership) 151

John 6: 1-15 (Some question Jesus even when he ministered to others) 151

John 6: 60-71 (Jesus being betrayed) 152

John 7: 2-5 (Jesus, even challenged by his own family member) 151-152

John 10: 22-39 (Jesus challenged by the Jewish Leadership) 151

John 10:10b (I come that you have life, and have it to the full) 14

John 14: 9-11 (Don't you know me?) 12

John 14: 12-14 (He will do greater things than these) 138-139

John 14: 12-14 (You may ask me for anything in my name, and I will do it) 174

John 14: 12-16 (And I will ask the Father and he will give you another Counselor)13

John 14: 12-16 (Anyone who has faith in me will do what I have been doing) 13

John 14: 23-27 (If anyone loves me, he will obey my teaching) 54

John 15: 1-4 (I am the true vine, and my Father is the gardener) 174

John 15: 1-8 (I am the true vine, and my Father is the gardener) 25,98

John 15: 1-8 (I am the vine, and you are the branches) 25

John 15: 9-13 (Now remain in my love) 7

John 18: 1-9 (Jesus being betrayed) 152

John 18: 10-11 (Disciple did not understand Jesus) 151

John 18: 15-17 (Jesus being denied) 152

John 19: 1-16 (Jesus attacked at his mocked trial) 152

John 20: 21-23 (Receive the Holy Spirit) 24

Luke 4: 1-13 (Satan Temps Jesus in the Wilderness) 150

Luke 4: 14-30 (Prophet not welcomed in his own town) 151

Luke 6: 38 (Give and it will be given to you) 65

Luke 7: 18-23 (John the Baptist had questions of Jesus) 151

Luke 8: 43-48 (Woman with an issue of blood) 99

Luke 9: 10-17 (Some question Jesus even when he ministered to others) 151

Luke 9: 51-56 (Disciple did not understand Jesus) 151

Luke 10: 1-7 (The harvest is plentiful, but the workers are few) 20

Luke 10: 29-35 (The good Samaritan) 7-8

Luke 10: 29-35 (Who is my neighbor) 7-8

Luke 12: 16-21 (Rich Young Ruler) 119

Luke 12: 31 (But seek [God] kingdom, and these thing will be given to you) 123

Luke 12: 34 (For where your treasure is, there your heart will be also) 123-124

Luke 12: 48 (For anyone who has been given much, much will be demanded) 116

Luke 17: 11-19 (10 men with Leprosy) 101-102

Luke 18: 1-5 (Widow and the Judge who never feared God) 92

Luke 18: 35-43 (Blind beggar) 100

Luke 19: 45-48 (Jesus challenged by the Jewish Leadership) 151

Luke 20: 1-8 (Jesus challenged by the Jewish Leadership) 151

Luke 21: 1-4 (this poor woman has put in more than all the others) 63

Luke 22: 1-6 (Jesus being betrayed) 152

Luke 22: 47-48 (Jesus being betrayed) 152

Luke 22: 49-53 (Disciple did not understand Jesus) 151

Luke 22: 54-62 (Jesus being denied) 152

Luke 23: 32-43 (Jesus being challenged on the cross) 152

Luke 23: 8-24 (Jesus attacked at his mocked trial) 152

Mark 6: 1-6 (Prophet not welcomed in his own town) 151

Mark 6: 30-44 (Some question Jesus even when he ministered to others) 151

Mark 8: 1-9 (Some question Jesus even when he ministered to others) 151

Mark 8: 36 (What profits a man to gain the world and forfeit his soul?) 124

Mark 9: 29 (This kind can come out only by prayer) 146

Mark 10: 17-27 (Good teacher) 57

Mark 10: 17-27 (Why do you call me good?) 57

Mark 11: 27-33 (Jesus challenged by the Jewish Leadership) 151

Mark 12: 29-31 (Love the Lord you God with all your heart, soul and mind) 6-7

Mark 12: 29-31 (Love your neighbor as yourself) 6-7

Mark 13: 43-52 (Jesus being betrayed) 152

Mark 14: 66-72 (Jesus being denied) 152

Mark 15: 16-39 (Jesus being challenged on the cross) 152

Matthew 4: 1-11 (Satan temps Jesus in the wilderness) 150

Matthew 5: 13-16 (You are the light of the world) 139

Matthew 5: 25-34 (Therefore I tell you, do not worry about your life) 55

Matthew 6: 16-18 (They have received their reward in full) 149

Matthew 6: 25-34 (Don't worry about your life) 147

Matthew 11: 1-6 (John the Baptist had questions of Jesus) 151

Matthew 12: 22-37 (Jesus was called a demon) 151

Matthew 13: 53-58 (Prophet not welcomed in his own town) 151

Matthew 14: 15-21 (Feeding of 5,000) 69

Matthew 14: 25-33 (The disciple displayed little faith) 151

Matthew 14; 6-14 (Jesus had no time to mourn, even for his cousin) 151

Matthew 17: 14-20 (If you have faith as small as a mustard seed) 28

Matthew 17: 14-20 (Nothing will be impossible for you) 28

Matthew 17: 21 (Howbeit this kind goeth not but by prayer and fasting) 28

Matthew 25: 14-30 (Parable of the Talents) 114

Matthew 25: 26-28 (You wicked, lazy servant!) 132

Matthew 25: 31-40 (Whatever you did for the one of the least of these) 129

Matthew 26: 47-50 (Jesus being betrayed) 152

Matthew 27: 11-26 (Jesus attacked at his mocked trial) 152

Matthew 27: 27-56 (Jesus being challenged on the cross) 152

Matthew 28: 16-20 (All authority in heaven and on earth has been given to me) 17

Matthew 28: 16-20 (Therefore go and make disciples of all nations) 17, 20-21

Philippians 4: 12-13 (I can do everything through him who gives me strength) 62

Philippians 4: 12-13 (I know what it is to be in need) 62, 83-84

Philippians 4:13 (I can do everything through him who give me strength) 135

Romans 1: 21-27 (Homosexuality) 106

Romans 7: 14-19 (For what I want to do I do not do, but what I hate I do) 97

Romans 10:9 (You will be saved) 145, 159

Romans 12: 1-2 (Offer your bodies as living sacrifices) 131

Romans 12: 2 (Be transformed by the renewing of your mind) 66

Romans 12:1 (Offer your bodies as living sacrifices, holy and pleasing to God) 33

Romans 13: 3 (Do what is right and he will commend you) 108

Romans 14: 12 (So then, each of us will give an account of himself to God) 116

Self-Esteem 171-174

Seventh-Day Adventist 41

Seven Percent Budgeted for Living Expenses 74

Sister So-n-so 163

Shadrach, Meshach, and Abednego (Daniel 3: 16-18) 108,109

Shakespeare's Romeo and Juliet 4

Sodium
    Diet 35-36
    Liquid Aminos 36

Sodom and Gomorrah 104-106 (Genesis 19:1-13) 106

Somebody Prayed for Me 163

Songs
    You Can't Beat God's Giving (Doris M. Akers) 63
    Never Would Have Made It (Marvin Sapp) 93-94
    Somebody Prayed for Me 163
    I Believe I Can Fly (R. Kelly) 178-179

Sound Social living (E.J. Ross) 161

Soy Protein 36

Speak in tongues (1 Corinthians 13: 1-13) 1

Spirit/Spiritual
    Basic Training (Matthew 4:1-11, Luke 4: 1-13) 149-150
    Gifts (Galatians 5: 16-25) 16
    Jesus wilderness experience (Matthew 4:1-11, Luke 4: 1-13) 149-150 Jesus spiritual

challenge 150-152 Walk in the spirit 16

Stress Control 146

Stewardship 14, 18, 63-70, 113-116, 122-126, 129-130
Christian Economics 70-75
Demonstrated 14
Gave an account 113-116
One who has been entrusted with much, much more will be asked (Luke 12:48) 116
Zone 86-87

Storge' 4

Stories & Experiences
Big Tip (Pregnant young woman) 26-27
Dominican Republic Youth Mission (Rev. Dr. Cecelia Williams Bryant) 30-31
Hobo on a Freight Train 172
Homeless Ministry experience 126-127
I Got My Degree 23-24
M.I.T. experience (Bishop John Richard Bryant) 137
Old lady and two devilish boys 140-141
Pregnant young woman 26-27
Rich Man – Poor Woman 9
The brother who stop tithing 122-123
The X (I Got My Degree) 23-24

Young man receiving a pink slip (Young man and the Rich Woman) 26-27

Stress Control 146-148

Study (2 Timothy 2: 15-16) 144-145

Sugar
Diet 37, 44
Triglyceride 37

Survival Techniques 64

T

Talents (Matthew 25: 14-30) 113-116

Task, Life's purpose 11

Teachers (Ephesians 4: 11-14) 140

Temple
Your body is a temple of God (1 Corinthians 3:16-17) 33
Your body is a temple of the Holy Spirit (1 Corinthians 6: 19-20) 34

Temptation
Jesus wilderness experience (Matthew 4:1-11, Luke 4: 1-13) 149-150

Ten percent to God by way of tithing 73

Ten percent to God's Servant (yourself) 73

Test
Health screening 40-41

The Good Samarian (Luke 10: 29-35) 8

The Great Commission (Matthew 28: 18-20) 20-21

The sheep and the Goats (Matthew 25: 31-40) 129

The Talents (Matthew25: 14-30) 113-114

The Way Movement 21

The Wilderness experience (Matthew 4: 1-11, Luke 4: 1-13)) 150

The Wright Brothers 138

The X (I Got My Degree) 23-24

Tithes
    Abram (Genesis 14: 18-20) 62
    Will a man rob God? (Malachi 3: 8-10) 64-65
    10 Percent to God 73

Tina Turner (What's love got to do with it?) 3

To inherit, you must recruit 19

Tongues, Speak in 1

Total earthly substance 64

Triglyceride
    Diet 37

True Vine (John 15: 1-8) 25

U

V

Vine
    Being connected (John 14: 12-14) 174

Veronique Dupree Chastain (Possible) 178

W

Warren Buffet 125, 127

Warren, Rick (Purpose Driven Church) 160

Watchman Nee 22

Water 35-36

Way Movement 21

Wealth
    God helps you (Deuteronomy 8: 18) 56
    Greed (Mark 8:36) 124
    Rich man (Mark 10: 17-27) 57

Seek first God's kingdom, and these things will be given to you as well (Luke 12: 31) 123
    The love of money (1 Timothy 6: 10a) 59

Who is my neighbor? (Luke 10: 29-35) 8

Wicked servant (Matthew 25: 26-28) 132

Widow/Widow's
    Mite 127

Wilderness experience (Matthew 4: 1-11, Luke 4: 1-13) 150

Winfrey, Oprah 125, 127

Witness
    Being a 17
    Dominican Republic 30-31
    Of a bank loan officer 23-24
    To inherit, you must recruit 19

Woman
    Devilish young boys

Issue of blood (Luke 8: 43-48) 99 With the non-fearing Judge (Luke 18: 1-5) 92

Wright Brothers 138

X

The X (I Got My Degree) 23-24

Y

Yahweh can be a SHE 15

You

  Are here for a purpose (Genesis 1:27-28) 11

  Are it 12

  Can't Beat God's Giving (Doris M. Akers) 63

Young

  Man in the bank with his degree 23-24

  Man receiving a pink slip (Young man and the Rich Woman) 26-27

  Rich Ruler (Mark 10: 17-27 57

Young pregnant woman 26-27

Your

  Body is a temple of God (1 Corinthians 3:16-17) 33

  Body is a temple of the Holy Spirit (1 Corinthians 6: 19-20) 34

Z

Further Reading

"American Debt Adviser," accessed http://americandebtadvisor.com.

American Institute for Cancer Research, retrieved from an advertisement article from of Peachtree City, GA: FC&A Publishing, 2013.

K.I. Barker, J.H. Stek, et al., eds. *Zondervan NIV Study Bible*, revised. Grand Rapids, MI: Zondervan, 2002.

Bryant, J.R. "A New Attitude." *The Anvil*, Nashville, TN: African Methodist Episcopal Church, 2011.

———. *Innovation*. Nashville, TN: African Methodist Episcopal Church, 2011.

Campbell, T.C., Campbell, T.M. *The China Study.* Dallas, TX: BenBella Books, Inc., 2006.

Chastain, V.D. *Possible.* Bloomington: Author House, 2011. (p. 47)

Dames, J.D. *The Church Member's Guide*. Nashville, TN: A.M.E. Sunday School Union, 2004.

Gelsey, R.C. *Imagine: A New Bible.* Good Hope Publishing Company, 1982.

Horovitz, B. "Want Health Food? Don't Eat Out." *USA Today*, May 17, 2012., p.1A.

Kail, R.V., Cavanaugh, J.C. *Human Development, A Life-Span View*, sixth edition. Belmont, CA: Wadsworth-Cengage Learning, 2013.

Kelly, R.S., Pires Do Nascimento, A., Marquinhos, M. *I Believe I Can Fly,* http://www.lyricsfreak.com/r/r+kelly/i+believe+i+can+fly_20113006.html.

Kotz, D. "Health & Lifestyle." *U.S. News & World Report, 82–83*, October 2009.

"Lumiday," https://www.lumiday.com/trial/?p=304

Miller, J.F. *Go Build a Church*. Winepress Publishing, 2007. (p.37)

Morgan, P., Lama, D. The Dalai Lama Sits Down with Piers Morgan, http://religion.blogs.cnn.com/2012/04/25/the-dalai-lama-sits-down-with-piers-morgan/

Nee, W. *Spiritual Authority*. New York: Christian Fellowship, 1972.

Nichols, D. *God's Plans for Your Finances*. Kensington, PA: Whitaker House, 1998.

Peale, N.V. *You Can If You Think You Can*. Pawling, NY: Foundation for Christian Living, 1974. (p.178)

Ross, E.J. *Sound Social Living*. Milwaukee, WI: Bruce Publishing, 1941. (p.122–123)

Sapp, M. "Never Would Have Made It." New York: Verity Records, a division of Sony Music Entertainment, 2006.

Spurgeon, C.H. "Footprints." *The Education of the Sons of God*, http://www.spurgeongems.org/vols46-48/chs2722.pdf

The Official King James Bible, http://www.kingjamesbibleonline.org/

Unknown. "The Don't Quit Poem," http://www.thedontquitpoem.com/thePoem.htm

Unknown. "*I Have Two Natures that Beat within My Chest,* http://fixednails.wordpress.com/2010/07/24/there-are-two-natures-that-beat-within-my-chest/

About the Author

E. J. Garrison was born in Detroit, Michigan, to the late Thomas and present Mother Emily Garrison. He was educated in the Detroit public schools and furthered his education by earning an Associate's degree from Highland Park Community College in Business Administration, a Bachelor's degree from Shaw College with a major in accounting. He then entered the M.B.A. program at the University of Detroit with a concentration in Economics & Statistics but his M.B.A. studies were short lived for God had other plans for his servant. Being obedient to his divine calling, E.J. Garrison enrolled at the Michigan Dieses of the Anglican Church School of Theology where he later earned his Deaconate Certification, which afforded him to study and graduate from SS. Cyril & Methodius Roman Catholic Seminary with his Master's in Religious Education.

His ministerial career began in 1982 when he was awarded his Exhorters License in the African Methodist Episcopal Church. He was ordained deacon in the A.M.E. in 1985 and immediately appointed assistant pastor at Bethel A.M.E. in Detroit. In 1991, Reverend Garrison was assigned to the pastorate at Quinn Chapel in Cassopolis, Michigan; and two years later assigned to the pastorate of New St. James in Detroit.

In 1994, God blessed the Reverend E. J. Garrison by touching the hands of the bishop to assign him to Pleasant Valley A.M.E. Church in Belleville, Michigan. During that time, he taught Religious Studies at Marygrove College in Detroit. After five years, Reverend Garrison was assigned to St. Matthew A.M.E. Church in Detroit where he had the pleasure of pastoring the late Mother of Civic Rights, Mother Rosa Parks. In 2003, he was moved to the historic Newman Church in Pontiac, and to Vernon Chapel A.M.E. Church in the city of Flint in 2004. While serving in Flint, he was appointed trustee on the Board of Flint Public Library.

In 2011, E. J. Garrison was assigned to the pastorate of Wayman A.M.E. Church in Racine, Wisconsin, where he served at the time of this publication.

He also served as:

Director of Christian Education for the Michigan Conference, which is part of the 4th Episcopal District of the African Methodist Episcopal Church

Church School Superintendent for the 4th Episcopal District

Coordinator for the Certification Program of the Department of Christian Education of the A.M.E. Church

FOR WORKSHOPS, TRAINING AND OTHER APPEARANCES, PLEASE E-MAIL US AT:

GarrisonMinistry@aol.com
or mail us at
P.O. Box 081485
Racine, WI 53408

Made in the USA
Charleston, SC
20 July 2013